"I laughed, I cried, I everythinged."

— Maryanne Covalence

"Joanne's story of growing up in a boisterous loving Italian family is both endearing and heartwarming. It's wonderful being reminded of the old fashioned ways that we've already forgotten about in our fast paced lives of today. Read about being raised in the 50's and 60's and have a wonderful nostalgic trip — or see how simple and fun childhood used to be. Her family was so full of love you will be moved to tears of laughter and sadness all in the same sitting! Simply a lovely story."

— Toni Allocco

"The mind is the heart of the memory...
This line expresses how rich and how important our "bank of memories" from our childhood affects each of us...
Joanne, thanks for the simplicity of mind and for sharing such wonderful parents."

— Regina N. Quintans

"What a treasure of a book! The story is personal and heartfelt, and yet it is so engaging and full of love it makes me wish I had been a member of the family."

— Deborah Graham

For the Love of Wood

By Joseph DiGiovanna's Daughter
Joanne Ferreri

authorHOUSE®

AuthorHouse™
1663 Liberty Drive
Bloomington, IN 47403
www.authorhouse.com
Phone: 1-800-839-8640

First published by AuthorHouse 9/7/2011

ISBN: 978-1-4567-5556-0 (sc)
ISBN: 978-1-4567-5558-4 (hc)
ISBN: 978-1-4567-5557-7 (e)

Library of Congress Control Number: 2011908703

Printed in the United States of America

This book is printed on acid-free paper.

With special thanks and love to my dear friends and family.

Janet Petronella, who unlocked the flood-gate of emotion in my soul that had been imprisoned far too long which allowed me just to begin.

Maryanne Covalence, Toni Allocco and Regina N. Quintans who listened with a full heart and open soul to all my stories and read every page of this book to ensure the love for my parents came through.

The Heaven sent Deborah Graham, who appeared just as I had given up on creating the book of my dreams. When everyone said it was impossible, her magical skills helped me to print the pages upside down and finally see the finished book exactly as I envisioned it.

To my Earth Angels, my children: Anne - proof reader extraordinaire and Joseph - photographer of the treasures, who lovingly provided the final touches.

Special thanks to my favorite sister and best friend Lillian Coloreo ('Lil) who supported me with love and money to help make this book a reality.

♥♥♥

Can you imagine having the vision to see a car in a block of wood, a church steeple in a burned out Roman candle or an entire wall-to-wall library from discarded window shutters? The only person I ever met that could, was my Dad. From a pile of garbage, he could imagine and create gold – treasures, trinkets and toys – memories of a lifetime and heirlooms for generations.

This book is written for you, so that even though you may never have had the personal pleasure of meeting him or touching one of his creations, you may indeed come to love him. This book could have been entitled "The Man that Everyone Instantly Loved." In memory of my Dad, the man of pure love, the love of my life, my first boy friend and lifelong hole in my soul now that he has graduated to Heaven.

Table of Contents

The Man Who Never Angered

Dad was a quiet man. He rarely got angry. My only real memory of him being angry was when I was in kindergarten and everyone was running after Joel. Joel was so cute. He had thick, dark curly hair and one day the girls in my class just started to chase him in the school yard after lunch. So, I did too! Being the person I am, I ran to catch him. I ran fast! I tripped and ripped my new leotards! Oh my God, Mom was going to kill me. I didn't even care that I tore into my knee, scrapped it badly and it was bleeding! The rest of the day is a blur, until I got home. How was I going to tell Mom and what was she going to do to me? It must have been my lucky day. Mom was preoccupied, probably with dinner. My Mom always made great dinners and this time she asked Dad to administer my punishment and to be tough about it. I remember he took me into their sacred bedroom with the highly polished wooden floors. The bowling alley wax that they used made the floors so slippery that you could slip and hurt yourself. *Little did they know that I often ran in, landed on the scatter rugs that edged the bed and took off on my magic carpet like Aladdin.*

Dad sat me down on a bench from their post World War II bedroom set, with the inlay wood and round mirror on the vanity. He was probably more nervous than I was. Dad didn't have a mean bone in his body. There was what seemed to be an eternity of silence as he paced the floor of his bedroom, and then he said with a slightly higher pitch, "Don't do it again, Boobie. Let's go eat dinner." Then he gave me a kiss and the look, the look we alone shared to his last day on earth. The silent, "I love you more than anything, you are my baby."

Wow, what could I do after that terrible lashing? The only thing I could. It was the last time I followed the crowd. If I knew then what I know now, I would have found a quiet time when not too many people were near us. I would have told Joel that he was cute and maybe we would have shared a Good Humor® Ice Cream from Rocky the ice cream man that came to our school every day. *Rocky, one of the men in my life I will never forget. How could I? He could do a trick and split his thumb in half. Even if we thought we knew how he did it; we watched it every day.*

Dancing on His Feet

I learned to dance from my Dad. Dancing on his feet at weddings – I guess I was a little jealous when he danced with Mom in the living room on Sundays waiting for the gravy to cook. I often got a turn, learning after Mom. My earliest memories, I must have been 3 or 4 and I would carefully place my feet on top of his and just get swept away by him in the music. This was only practice. The true test of our skill was to dance at weddings. When I was young it seemed that we were always going to weddings. It was a magical time – the innocence of youth and the comfort of my father's strong hands and arms as I glided across the dance floor.

The Sunday Comics in Bed

I know that Sundays are sacred. If anything was a close second, it was Mom and Dad's bed. Every day, Mom would make it carefully with love, pulling the bottom sheet tight, no wrinkles, with tucked army corners. You could have bounced a quarter off the top. On the other hand, my bed which I shared with my sister Lillian was often used as a trampoline and the basis for many pillow fights. It was rare that I was even allowed in their bedroom. I rarely even touched the sacred bed except when I was asked to help make it and when I was invited in by Dad to read the Sunday Comics with him. I must have been only three or four years old; I only remember that I couldn't read yet and that it was a real treat. I would watch Dad in bed from the corner of my eye as I sat on the couch in the living room in my PJs watching cartoons, The East Side Kids, or The Three Stooges. Dad and I always had a silent communication between us. *I always regretted that we didn't talk in detail about all kinds of subjects: Mom, life, death, the afterlife after he lived with me for five years when Mom passed.* I realize now, we didn't have to talk. Our unique silent communication of love probably began with reading the Sunday Comics in bed. I would watch Dad from the corner of my eye read all the boring stuff; you know all the stuff that was in black and white. The Sunday Daily News was huge. He always carefully and methodically removed all the sections first. The top section, the black and white News, went to Dad. I never remember Mom reading the news section. She just glanced at it and went right to the Obituaries and Ann Landers for advice. I think that sometimes she would send in a question and anxiously flip past any story regarding the horrors of world that may have occurred the night before, to get to Ann Landers. The ads for sending away for stuff always got thrown out, except for the Haband™ advertisement; both of my parents were big on comfort clothes of polyester and spandex.

Next, all the store ads were sorted like Sears and Macys to check for sales on stuff that we might be looking to buy. The Parade section was like a weekly magazine of articles of general interest scattered with some black and white comics, boring for a three year old no matter how

3

funny they might have been. Finally, the real comics were left. The color comics; the ones that would leave multicolor dye all over your hands if they were damp; the ones you could press Silly Putty® on and have the comics come off in reverse. How cool. Who cared if the words were in reverse, I couldn't read anyway. I would press flattened Silly Putty on to the page, lift it off and stretch the comic to what seemed to me as a little kid to be 50 feet and was most likely only 5 inches!

Dad's eyes would peer over the top of the newspaper. He knew I had been watching him. I knew that he knew I had been watching him. He would slowly, what seemed to be an eternity, put down the paper, lift up Mom's side of the sheets and I knew that was the silent signal for me to read the comics with him. I would run as quickly as I could in my PJs with the plastic feet in them. Remember, I had to be very careful because their wooden floor was polished with bowling alley wax for that super slippery shine. I would carefully leap into the comfort of their sacred bed, but more importantly into the comfort of my Dad's arms and watch anxiously as he read every single comic to me. I loved it Dad, thank you for the sacred memories of Sunday Comics.

The Most Beloved Supervisor

Before there were the hundreds of uppity, expensive management tools, tricks of the trade, gurus galore to see how much work you could legally get out of your employees, there was Dad. Dad had the unique ability to be pure love, to instantly see through whatever faults are in you, whatever evil is in you and whatever traits you have, and say, "That's just the way he is", or if you were really.bad he would say that you were "An I don't know what" and he loved you anyway, instantly. This was most evident with the people that he managed at the Post Office Garage. I can't imagine Dad being mean to anyone. I can't even imagine him telling anyone what to do. He rose from the ranks of mechanic after WWII to supervisor at the garage. I could see him now, "Just go do what you know that you have to," he would probably say. Even though I'm sure there were work assignments, paperwork and deadlines. Dad probably never gave orders or yelled. If on occasion he was forced to, I'm sure it was in a quiet tone and very respectfully to the person he addressed.

I learned firsthand just how much he was loved when he retired. Everyone, from the most senior in his department, to the newest and youngest mechanic in his care, loved and respected Dad. The youngest mechanic was a far cry from the other rugged post-WWII men. He was small, thin and had taken etiquette classes. He wore gloves when he repaired the trucks. It didn't matter; they all respectfully hugged Dad and individually told him just how much they were going to miss him. **Listen, all you fancy management gurus, here's the secret to getting what you need from your employees – genuinely, love and respect them.**

I guess now that the first time I knew Dad was a special kind of supervisor was at Christmas time. He and Mom would sit at the kitchen table and write out and send individual Christmas cards to everyone who was in Dad's care. Dad's care, that's it. Since he loved them, they didn't work for him; he just took care of them. I remember the list being very long. Mom always had very religious Christmas cards and bought some generic Holiday Greetings. Dad would sit next to her and say, "This person needs a generic one." Mom would write them out individually and personally, no return labels, no fancy computer script written envelopes and no card store pre-typed ones. Mom had the best handwriting and Dad could lick stamps and seal envelops at lightning speed. There were no pre-glued stamps either. Actually, I remember Dad using the Post Office trick of a dampened sponge in a bowl rather than using his tongue. After they were done with their activity of love, there would always be a shoe box full of neatly addressed and stamped cards in size order. Then they would start on the huge list of family Christmas cards to be sent out. This is a lost labor of love at a time when stamps were 3¢ and family activities were done around the kitchen table. Today, I go to an animated site for Christmas cards, cut and paste hundreds of email addresses in the BCC column of my email and I'm done. How sad.

Christmas was another time when he touched us with his love for wood. We have always had the same simple knick knack holder in every house we have lived in. It's always been hung in a fairly prominent place. The holder now is on the wall of the entrance to my home. Luckily, one day I asked Dad about it.

"I never told you, Boobie? You know all the times you didn't see me much right before Christmas?"

"Yeah, I guess so," I responded.

"I was working overtime at the Post Office. One, because we had to make sure all the trucks were working properly in order to ensure that the Christmas cards and presents would be delivered."

Wow! I just realized Dad was probably single handedly responsible for the post office motto "Neither rain, nor sleet, nor dark of night will keep the mailman from delivering the mail!"

He told me that the second reason he worked overtime was to have extra money to buy me toys. *That I understood much better.*

He said that the knick knack holder was made a long time ago during his overtime before Christmas when there wasn't much going on. He made it from the old running boards discarded from the trucks. He designed it himself and made it in the repair shop.

Roman Candles - Burnt Offering - Church Cross

Dad never wasted anything and I mean ANYTHING. He was brought up during the depression. There were six kids in the family, three boys and three girls. Now that I think of it, the small apartment they all lived in behind my Grandpa's barbershop on Grand Street in Brooklyn was very small. I think that there were only two bedrooms. Dad told me that they would have to share EVERYTHING. The only thing he really minded sharing, even though they were washed were his brother's socks. *Apparently one of his brothers was not very clean…*back to the story.

It was the 4th of July. Certain fireworks were illegal but luckily we lived next to a police officer who had spent most of the previous months confiscating the illegal ones, you know the really good stuff. His house was filled! Our 4th was spent on the porch and stoop watching and holding our ears from early morning until the Roman candles at night. Macy's display had nothing on our neighbor's display! One time the neighbor's son came out with a huge roll of something. It looked like the Rambo roll of ammo that fed the machine gun. It was at least two feet in diameter made up of double fire crackers tied together at the fuses. Instead of laying it flat and lighting it like a fuse from a keg of dynamite, he somehow threw it up and over the power line. There hanging, at least a story high on each side was hundreds maybe even thousands of firecrackers! The neighbors all watched in silence and awe. He lit the end. Bada Bing Bada Bang, Bada Bing Bada Bang, it was cool to watch the firecrackers go off alternating right to left and back again for what seemed to be an eternity. Then it reached the halfway mark and the weight of the lit versus unlit was too much and CRASH, the unlit all fell to a huge pile and exploded in one BIG BOOM! I can imagine what it must feel like on the front line of a battle field.

The following day, when all was done and the smoke lifted, even though the block was still smoldering, Dad went to look for something in the debris that he might be able to use someday, sometime, somewhere. He saved a lot of stuff that he might be able to use someday, sometime, somewhere. I still have a lot of the stuff. He picked up the charred remains of Roman candles.

"Dad, what in the world are you going to do with that?" I asked.
"I'm not sure yet, but I'll figure something out," he replied.

And figure it out he did. This time he made very good use of what he found.

Years later, Secret Santa, that's what some younger kids on our block used to think he was, got busy in his shop. He immerged with what appeared to be many small homes. He proudly and carefully – since everything had to be the way he knew you wanted it, even though you may have pictured it otherwise, laid out two entire villages of homes, one for me and one for my sister. Dad loved us both so much that he always made two of everything. We would always love and treasure whatever he made. My brother is another story. More of a perfectionist than my Dad, Matty didn't always get a set of Dad's creations. So Dad set out the houses, each uniquely hand painted, but one was very special. It stood proudly in the center of the village. It was the cornerstone, the church and proudly atop the steeple was a fragile cross, made from the remains of the 4th of July's debris. How ironic the charred remains of a Roman candle became the cross for a church, the church that is the focal point for my Christmas village every year.

Traditions

Grand Street in Brooklyn has been the home of many different immigrant groups. My family's turn was when I was growing up. 796 Grand Street was the home of my Grandparents and my Grandfather's barbershop. If I close my eyes, I can see the barber pole outside the small two-seat storefront. Later, my Uncle Jimmy would carry on the tradition of his Dad. It was our tradition to go every Sunday after our feast of Meat Gravy (that's what Italian's call real homemade tomato sauce) and right after Mom scrapped the cold and hardened grease from the crevices of the old stove, which had inevitably spilled from the bubbling gravy. Little did anyone think then that same grease would eventually have to be scraped from their arteries.

Many years later, Dad's sister, Aunt Josie, was diagnosed with breast cancer. She reluctantly had her breasts removed. I spoke with her in the hospital and promised to come and see her when she returned to Grand Street. The same Grand Street of my youth and it hadn't changed a bit. The only thing different this time was that I was armed with a camera. This time I was preserving a memory on paper for generations rather than just in my heart. Dad and I visited together and when we pulled up to the house at 796 the memories of "the every Sunday after sauce visits" seeped into the core of my being. Everything was different of course. My Grandparents were gone. Aunt Faye, Uncle Charlie, Uncle Danny and Bootsie, the dog, were all gone. My numerous cousins were all married with children of their own. However, Uncle Jimmy, the oldest of 3 brothers, was still religiously in Grandpa's barbershop as he had been every day for over 40 years. Aunt Josie, the oldest of the 3 sisters was still on the 3rd floor of a 3 story – 6 family tenement that belonged to my Grandparents. The only home she knew in addition to the one she was born in around the corner. How simple life was then.

Immediately, visions raced through my head of family gatherings – numerous baptisms, communions, confirmations, pre-weddings, post mass before the receptions gathering and unfortunately the post wake and burial gatherings – in spite of the reason, they were pretty much the same. At least 50 people, you know just the immediate family and their kids, not counting Gasper the Pot Man, or Millie the Tenant, or the 2nd and 3rd cousins, all of whom lived two blocks away and looked like clones of my Dad, and were all named Joseph (Giuseppe DiGiovanna), crammed into the three very small railroad rooms. *"Railroad rooms" is the name given to the layout of an apartment where all the rooms line up in a straight line, one after the other, usually without a door, having only an archway between them.* The coats were piled high on Aunt Faye's bed. Cousin Matty, Joey and Louis's bedroom, which was really a hall, was transformed into a feast. Trays of assorted Italian cold cuts, rolled so thin that you could use them as a straw, braided egg rolls and of course the centerpiece which was a whole turkey that mysteriously had always been surgically carved and placed back on the bone with all the skin intact. The claw legged tub that was in the bathroom down the hall, with the single 20 watt bulb and no lamp shade, was loaded with huge chunks of ice and soda. Dessert was always the horrible cassata cake – a pretty decent plain cake with cannoli filling that got ruined by soaking the bottom layer in rum! Hmmm, perhaps that was to help the all too many cousins who ran wild up and down three flights of apartments calm down so that all the adults who ignored our antics could play cards for hours on end. The adults perpetually yelled all night for what many would have assumed to be blood money, when in reality they bet with pennies.

Armed with my camera, I snapped picture after picture of the barbershop, which was the same as I remember from the time we all got our first hair cut from my Grandfather. Now it was void of customers, yet Uncle Jimmy stood proudly and patiently at the front door just in case. I went to the backyard where the fig tree, which began from a cutting of my Grandfather's tree in Italy, still stood. It was two stories high. Then I went to Aunt Josie's apartment and stood in awe in front of the living room lamps with the colonial dancing couple base which were well over fifty years old yet brand new because they were still covered in plastic. The piano that my cousins Rosemary and Charlotte might have played once or twice as children was now totally covered in their children's baby pictures alongside their own baby pictures.

The memories were incredibly vivid. Yet a new one will never leave my soul. I was brought to the basement. If I thought the house was scary, the basement was terrifying. A single 20 watt bulb would have been a blessing. There were no lights and the rickety, slanting, wooden stairs would not have passed today's housing inspection. There was no railing, so not to fall; you carefully felt your way along the pointy stucco wall going down the stairs. Uncle Jimmy waited upstairs in the barbershop in case a customer came in. Aunt Josie, Dad and I, descended the stairs and went from one room to another dark clammy cold room. Dad was in his glory. I'm sure he was re-living a time long ago when he played games with his sisters and brothers in these rooms. But why was I there? Dad took me to a small alcove; I can't be sure because I couldn't see very well. Our only light was what came in from the street through the very dirty windows that edged the basement ceiling. He wanted me to see something.

He said, "You know Boobie, the mallet that Mom uses to pound veal cutlets for spadines?"

"Yea, I guess so." I replied.

"Well this is the work bench where I made it. Way before your Mom, I sanded it all by hand right here. It was the first wooden thing I made as a kid. It's where I made the manger out of a discarded cigar box, too."

WOW, Dad brought me to the SHRINE, the place where all his lifelong projects of wood began. I was honored and really wanted to take a serious long look and couldn't. I wanted a picture of this! I foolishly asked if there was a light that could be turned on. Right! No such luck. I said to Dad that I really want to see it.

He said, "That's ok, just touch it, it will be enough."

I did and it was.

I still have and use the mallet.

Here are some of the oldest and dearest pictures
I have of my Dad's parents and his siblings.

Grandpa Matteo DiGiovanna
1890

My paternal grandparents, Calogera and Matteo DiGiovanna on their wedding day in 1907 or at least when they took the picture. My Aunt Mary said that Grandpa had shaved his mustache for the wedding and that my Grandma refused to take an official wedding picture until it grew back a few months later, so she is actually pregnant in this photo.

Grandma
June 22, 1929

Jim, Grandpa, Joe
June 22, 1929

Playing cards
1930

Our gang
November 11, 1931
Aunt Mary with the cigarette
Dad is at the top of the gang.

Our gang again
November 11, 1931
Find Uncle Jimmy & Uncle Charlie
(L) Cousin Charlie, who later married Dad's sister Faye, is next to
his brother Jimmy, and my Grandmother. My Dad is on the right.

June 18, 1933

June 18, 1933
Jim, Charlie and Joe

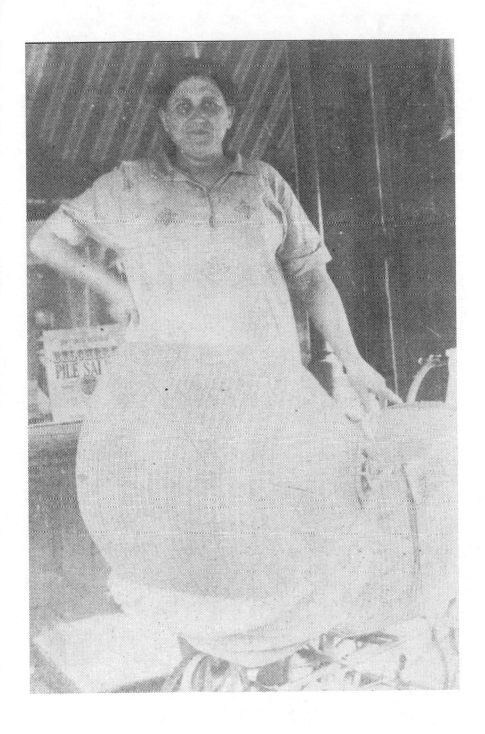

July 22, 1937
Mary & Grandpa

Very young and very handsome Dad

Joe, Tony & Jim

Grandma outside the barbershop.

Mattes Sai Giavonine   *Calogera Digio Vanna*

All grown up – 1984
RIGHT – Uncle Jimmy, Aunt Mary, Aunt Faye, Aunt Josie,
Dad, Uncle Tony in inset
LEFT – Uncle Jimmy, Auntie Anne, Aunt Josie, Uncle Danny,
Mom, Dad, Uncle Adrian, Aunt Mary and Aunt Faye

Dad picking figs in the
back yard like he did as
a child, from the fig tree
that his father brought
over from Italy.

Building a House - Anne's Doll House

When I was growing up, I can remember that both of my parents seemed to have unbounded energy. Mom would always be cooking, cleaning or working. Dad would always be working, which seemed to come second to whatever project he was doing in the basement. He was always fixing or maintaining something for the house; he took great pride in our house.

719 E. 31ˢᵗ Street

1958   *1980*

Our house was really a home, it was not big at all by today's standards, but it was large enough to hold the unbridled and steadfast love of both of my parents. The house was a two-family, the staple of that proverbial extra income which I'm sure helped many a time, even though the apartment was rent controlled. All five of us lived on the top floor, Mom, Dad, my sister Lillian and brother Matty. Five people lived in five rooms and shared one bathroom. It is not imaginable by today's standard that each family member would have a set time to use the bathroom or you would be out of luck. In a dire emergency, one would venture down two flights of stairs to the ominous basement, take our dog, Fluffy, for protection and use the bathroom next to Dad's workshop. The only time the bathroom was cleaned was if we were having company. All of the spare folding chairs for parties were stored in the shower stall. My current friends, with a family of four, have at least five or six bathrooms in their house and there is constant fighting because one sibling doesn't want to use the bathroom next door!

Now, back to the story of Dad's pride in our home. Dad always fixed or maintained something in the house, whether it was scrapping and repainting the entire outside, laying linoleum squares in the basement, fixing electrical outlets or caring for the vegetable garden. Come to think of it, we never had repairmen for anything; Dad did it all. Somehow, without any formal education in any trade, Dad was a jack of all. Dad's health began to fail. I believe it was in the early 70's, when he had his first heart attack. I remember being so scared. I realized for the first time just how fragile life really is. Thank God he pulled through. Years later, after helping me move into my second home, he had another heart attack. Unable to do heavy wood projects, at least for a while, we all tried to figure out what could keep Dad busy. He was retired now; my siblings and I were all married and my parents moved into a four-room house. So Mom and Dad's primary activity was to go food shopping and maintain a safe distance between each other to prevent agita (aggravation).

Finally, I came up with an idea. I asked Dad to build my daughter, Anne, a house! Not as big as 719, but just as detailed. Dad built Anne a dollhouse. What a great idea! From scratch and with great love, Anne became the recipient of a beautiful three story Colonial. Dad, good old Dad, nothing was second best. He built it from scratch, painted it, laid down the flooring and carpeting, put up the wallpaper, installed room to room electricity and built the entire antique bathroom! Section by section we would go shopping together in the mini–Home Depot®, a.k.a. doll house store, to shop. Luckily for Anne, and me, both Grandmothers were in competition to see who could spoil her more, and so they paid for most of the incredibly cool miniatures.

It was good to hear of his progress.

"Boobie, today I put the roof on an entire house."

The roof was the only aspect of the house that Dad and I disagreed on. Being the gifted math genius, I calculated perfectly just how many shingles were needed based upon the size of the roof and spread of the shingles. Dad insisted on spreading them out a lot more than necessary not to waste them. He spread out the shingles to save the extra. We had a lot extra, but all packages were opened. I couldn't return them.

"Maybe we could use them elsewhere," he said.

Where in the world was I going to use ½" by ¼" shingles? Is anyone out there building a dollhouse? To this day, almost 20 years later I still have the small zip lock bag that holds the extra shingles, just in case.

The Treasured Albums
That Hold My Memories

Dad firmly believed that anything could be made of wood and not just any wood, free wood. Sometimes I would want something and ask him to make it for me. The instructions would call for a certain type or grain or thickness of wood which was appropriate for the project and Dad would just go to his pile of separated dresser drawers and grab a piece. Case in point, I was getting married and I saw a picture of a wooden album in a magazine. I showed Dad the picture and he said,

"No problem, Boobie," he always said that to me no matter what I wanted.

So, from the picture I showed him, sprang the proverbial plethora of thick, very heavy duty, last for generations' wooden albums; some for me, some for my sister and some for my brother. Each had Dad's special touch. He had learned to groove lettering in the wood and add 3–D shapes. So now I am truly blessed with his wooden treasures that hold my family treasures, our pictures.

The Hidden Treasures He Left Behind

Dad worked with love and never asked for a penny for his efforts. However, he was always rewarded. We had great neighbors when we left our home at 719. Maryann & Tony lived in a circa house next door; right after Lenny and Helen whose house was attached to ours. On a narrow block in Brooklyn, with attached homes and cement back yards, their house took up the space for at least 3 homes! So by Brooklyn standards, it was huge and it was the perfect match for both the current owners and my parents.

The first thing my Dad said was that he had to see the inside of the house. Since the outside was made of wooden shingles surrounded by a wooden picket fence, he could only imagine what wooden treasures awaited within and they did. Long story short, Maryann and Tony as well as their two children Michael and Antonia all became best friends with my family. Since my parents were retired, they were always home and became a welcomed built-in sitter or extra set of grandparents. The kids would stop in to see my Mom for a snack and stop in to see what was being made in my father's new workshop, the attached garage.

Although our families grew to love each other as if we were blood relatives; we often went to each other's family functions and both children were in my bridal party; I know that their circa house became a special "friend" to my Dad. He explored every inch of every room, imagining all the history that had taken place over the last 150+ years. So when he was asked to do a little work in the house for them, he jumped on the opportunity. I don't really remember the details of what he did inside, but I do remember what he did to the inside of the inside! I believe he closed off a wall and made a different entrance in the kitchen. When he had the opportunity to bare the studs between the walls, he put in a time capsule. Actually, it was a Chock full o'Nuts ® coffee can. I don't know what was in it, but I'm sure there was a piece of Dad that he wanted to be remembered by, that someday will be revealed to another loving family.

I just remembered that we did the same time capsule in the walls of my bedroom at our home at 719! I remember signing my name to a piece of paper as a little kid then and Dad placed it in a can with some other memorabilia and placed it in the wall before he sealed it up. Maybe that was Dad's way of remaining immortal. Hopefully this book will help his wish.

The Treasures I Left Behind

In addition to the treasures Dad left behind in Brooklyn, when I moved from my first house to where I live now, I had to leave pieces of Dad's love for others to treasure. I know there were others, and that when we left one place to go to another, Dad always took everything that wasn't nailed down, including everything that was nailed down that didn't require removal of a major structure. However in my Fanwood home I had to sadly leave two major structures that I loved.

The first was my custom breakfast nook. It was one of those things I didn't know I needed, however, Dad knew and made it a perfect fit. Dad's labors of love always had something special. In the case of the breakfast nook, he cushioned removable seats so that the entire base that sat at least 6-8 people, became a storage area. It was great, especially because we had our first child, Anne, by then. The extra space held many toys.

The second treasure I sadly had to leave was my custom wall- to-wall library. I always wanted a library because I loved to read and had many books. I also wanted a place to proudly display every Charlie Brown paperback that was printed up until that time and all my science fiction books, especially my Asimov collection. Dad knew, in our silent communication, exactly what I wanted. So, after one of my excursions from garbage day in Fanwood, Dad knew exactly what to do with the custom oak shutters I acquired. Actually, I don't believe that they can be considered garbage. I remember driving around the neighborhood and a woman was walking out of her home carrying wooden shutters. I asked her what they were and she told me, "I hate to throw these custom shutters out. They are oak and were very expensive." I asked her to bring them directly to my car and assured her that they would go to very good use. Since they never touched the ground, technically they were not garbage. I really wasn't sure what I was going to do with them. Dad knew immediately, and said, "Don't worry Boobie; I know exactly what you want." I never worried and the result was a wall-to-wall library with cabinets across the bottom with wooden shutters for doors. "Thank you Dad." I hope the current owners appreciate the treasures I had to leave behind.

Anne inside her deer treasure holder.

Anne riding her rocking horse.

Clothespins Come Alive

As Dad got older and survived multiple illnesses and operations, we were always worried that he might hurt himself while building or lifting something that he was making. My sister, Lillian, was always looking for him to make something lighter. She found these adorable deer figurines that could be made from clothespins. Now Dad was always reluctant to try something that he hadn't thought of himself, but since this craft was made of wooden clothespins I guess he decided that it was all right. My sister provided the clothes pins and goggley eyes. Dad's new obsession took off. Once Dad decided, he always seemed obsessed with what he was doing and would spend what seemed like every waking moment that he wasn't eating, doing the task.

The deer were no exception. It began with the example that was in the directions and developed into deer families. He learned that the wooden clothespins came in miniature and that if he sanded different sections they would look more realistic. Dad played no favorites. All three of his children and his seven grandchildren always got a set of whatever he made. The deer families were adorable and instantly became part of the prized Christmas collection that will be handed down for generations.

The simple deer developed into different farm animals, like cows with utters and animals with felt blankets.

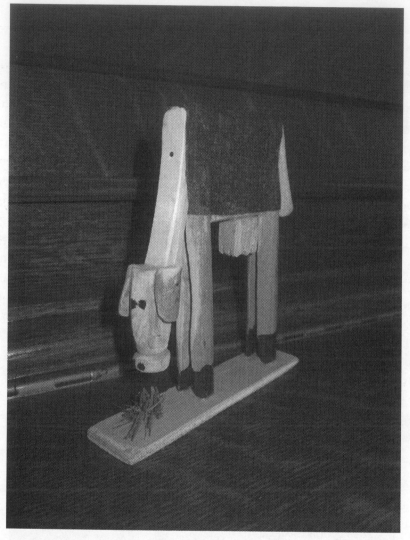

They were often given as gifts, a piece of love from Dad. One of our neighbors in Brooklyn, Lenny, was given a deer as a get-well gift because he was in the hospital. I understand that he clung to the deer with tears in his eyes because he knew my Dad loved him.

7-Foot Planter Upon a Green Hornet

Dad always knew what I needed, even when I didn't. He rarely asked and just made it. We were in our current home which has an acre of land. It is much bigger than the square cement backyard that I grew up with. Dad's eyes lit up when he saw the property. I'm sure that visions of fig trees, Sicilian bat squash and tomato vineyards danced in his head. Little did either of us realize that the creatures that came with our property ate everything! The first year we moved in, Dad came with a wooden trellis the type that grapes cling to and grow on. Magic seeds of 1-2 feet long Sicilian string beans were planted and what seemed to be overnight sprouted and climbed the trellis. The beans began to emerge, and then all of a sudden they stopped growing. But why did they stop growing? Then we noticed, carefully, as if by surgical scissors, the vines were cut

along the entire bottom. We had new neighbors under the shed. A family of rabbits moved in and invited themselves to the veggie buffet. That was the first and last time we ever even saw the magic beans again. We did get a few good years of tomatoes.

Dad didn't drive to any places that were far away from their house in Brooklyn. So it was a shock when he drove to my house in New Jersey. The only other place that I ever remember Dad driving far was to my Aunt Mary's and Uncle Adrian's, who live in Strasburg, Pennsylvania, near the Amish. Perhaps, it was the one time when I was young and Dad missed the turn onto the highway to go home from Pennsylvania that ruined him for life to drive very far. As young as I was, I was the only person in the car who knew how to read a map, so I told Dad that I could direct him to the next exit. I was an adventurous child, so I directed the entire carload of relatives, there had to be seven or eight of us squished in to our sedan. Thank God there were no seat belts or we wouldn't have fit! I thought that a slight detour to Gettysburg to see the site of the historic battle might be nice. So, an hour or so later, there we were staring at a field. I wasn't allowed to get out because they didn't understand the significance and thought I might get hurt. I conceded and guided the carload of relatives to the next exit. I think it was from this experience that Dad became a little reluctant to venture very far from Brooklyn.

So, when he drove to my house in New Jersey, one would have thought I moved to Mars, it became a trek. My parents would drive in sections, stopping along the way to gain perspective of the route, which had been carefully laid out for them. They had snacks prepared by Mom and I'm sure she was always balancing a Corningware® dish full of goodies for us on her lap. I'm sure there were many loud arguments in the car that I would have loved to be a fly on the proverbial wall to hear. It was a time before cell phones, so my Mom would always call right before they left the house and I would give it my best guess as to when they would reach each section of the route and arrive at my house.

On one visit, I was waiting for them outside when their car pulled into my driveway. What in the world was on top of the green Hornet? The Hornet, in case you don't know, was a short-lived car that was very small, not too pretty; ok it was ugly and had no pick up. This one in particular was green, the color Mom hated. Dad didn't buy it on purpose to get Mom angry, he bought it by accident at an auction in Brooklyn when he bid and won the wrong car. I could write an entire book on that argument alone!

So here come my parents; Mom running from the passenger seat, Corningware® in hand to get to the bathroom as quickly as possible and Dad removing this 7-foot thing from his roof. It was green of course anything that was for the outside was always 719 green. Even though Mom hated green; our first house at 719 was green. She justified not hating it by saying it was mint. There must have been some huge paint sale when they first bought the house after WWII because Dad never ran out of the paint, even though he scraped down the entire 719 house by hand and painted the two story home every few years. So here it is, the 1990s and Dad pulls up to my new house with this 7-foot thing, I still don't know what it is but it is 719 green so it must be for the outside and I need it, according to him. I learned early in life that Dad was always right, whether we agreed or not, so I didn't question that I needed this thing; I was just curious as to what it was.

Don't ask me how my now older Dad who had survived several heart attacks ever built this thing, got this thing on the roof of his small car or how he drove through two states and didn't get a ticket and how Mom let him must be another story, but here we were taking it off the roof. We walked to my small garden in the corner of my yard, it was the only haven we found that could grow tomatoes, and there we carefully placed the wooden flower box, which fit perfectly across all the windows and rested comfortably on some metal posts that I never even noticed.

It was exactly what I needed; I just didn't know it; "perfect Dad, thank you." The 7-foot planter was followed by many other treasures. Another one that I especially love is a high backbench with handmade hearts etched out in the back board.

Splitting the Curio Cabinet

Did you ever hear the story of wise King Solomon? God was supposed to have given him all the wisdom of the ages and his decisions were unsurpassed. There is a story that goes somewhat like this. Two women come to King Solomon and are having a horrendous argument between them. Since he is so wise, they agree to abide by his decision. Both women claimed to be the mother of a beautiful male newborn baby. Had there been hospitals at the time, I guess you might say it would have been a case of switching tags or mistaken identity at the hospital. It was more likely a case that both women were in the fields working twelve hour shifts and one had an on the job delivery and now both women were claiming possession of the blessed bundle. King Solomon was to be the proverbial and virtual blood test.

King Solomon wisely and silently listened to both women. Each presented a pretty good argument. He thought silently for a while, left the courtyard where they all had discussed the issue at hand and returned with an axe. "Ladies, each of you presented an equally convincing case. It is clear that either could be the mother. So, it is my decision to split the child in half and each of you can have a portion." In an instant, the first woman agreed that that would be fair. At the same instant, the other cried out in immediate grief and pain, shouting, "The first woman is the real mother, PLEASE, give the whole baby to her!" Solomon picked up the baby and handed it to the second woman.

King Solomon had nothing on Dad. I have a sister, Lillian, and Dad had an axe. SMACK! Split everything right down the middle whether or not either of us wanted the object. This is the story of the corner, or at least now it is, curio cabinet. Dad found a very pretty antique oak curio cabinet. It had four claw legs and a semicircular glass door. It was very pretty. Now, Lillian is much more feminine of the two of us and since I didn't even know what a curio cabinet was, I would have been perfectly happy if Lillian got the entire piece of furniture. But, I didn't have a choice. Dad decided we each needed one.

Now this was a one of a kind piece of furniture so wise Dad took out the axe, and I'm sure very carefully, split the curio in two and each of us now have a very unique ½ corner curio cabinet.

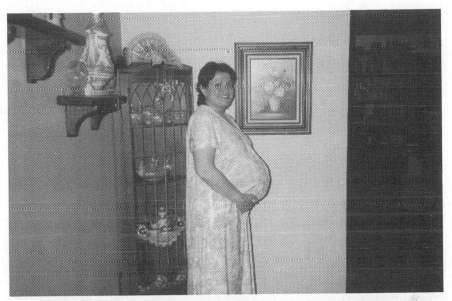

The cabinet became the focal point for very important pictures. Here I am in the top picture on the day I delivered Anne, April 29, 1988 and Joseph in the bottom picture, March 13, 1992.

Discarded Crib to Hand-Me-Down Cradle

I lived in Fanwood, New Jersey and drove only a few minutes to work each day. I was very fortunate to live so close. I often came home for lunch to eat with our dog Queenie. One morning, the traffic was routed away from the main street that took me directly to work. I was guided to side streets that I was never on and to Wood Heaven that I never could have imagined! At first it was surreal, I must have been dreaming. In front of every house was pile upon pile of goodies; furniture, toys, household items and especially wood of all shapes and sizes. It couldn't be true. What was all this stuff, which appeared to be still usable doing at the curb? I didn't ask questions. Having been blessed with the wood gene from my Dad, my eyes made a beeline for what appeared to be some sort of scrolled dowels. Wow, it was better than that, it was a beautiful crib all disassembled in a neat pile. I placed it in my car, went to work and came back later to see what else was available. New Jersey does things a little differently than the rest of the country. In New York when we threw out our garbage, the garbage men took it away. How novel, in New Jersey there are formal garbage days when you can throw out practically anything and you can do it a certain number of days before the designated pick up so that your friends and neighbors can have the pleasure of scrounging through it. The cradle experience was my 1st experience of a garbage day in Scotch Plains and definitely not my last. Dad and I got to be professionals. I would let him know when various towns were having their garbage days and we would go shopping together. Why not, the price was right and the treasures abounded. We had a ball! We were professionals. Armed with hammers, screwdrivers and an empty van, we drove in and out of all sorts of neighborhoods finding unbelievable treasures. In addition to wood, often oak, we found expensive brass knobs, new storm doors and exercise equipment. Since I don't do much garbage shopping because it's not fun anymore, I can reveal a tip to you.

One day you may pass a beautiful piece of furniture that you just can't take at the time or it won't fit in the car you are driving. You may say to yourself, "I'll come back later." Experience has proven to me that if it is at all usable, it will be gone. Take the drawers! No one will want a piece of furniture without the drawers and you can come back later, fully assured that it will be there. It's like putting a deposit in a rare find at an expensive furniture store and they just hold it for you with a tag that says "SOLD – Will be picked up later" with your name on it. We used to run into fellow garbage cruisers and when they came across a piece of furniture that was missing drawers, I know they must have seen the virtual sign, "Joe's Been Here – Be Back Later."

My sister thought we were nuts and we didn't care. One day she was with us and we stopped at a pile of neat brown boxes. "What are you doing?" She exclaimed. "That's filthy!" Dad and I opened a few boxes and said, "Lil, you may be interested in this." Boxes of new ceramics all neatly packed in tissue paper, some painted some not, and some Hummel's! What a find. I think we may have made a convert of my sister that day. We discovered a 12" high unpainted ceramic nativity set that she painted white and uses every Christmas. I miss our excursions. "Dad; it's not the same without you." When I pass a pile of stuff on garbage day I just drive by because the Wood Visionary is not with me.

Back to the story about the first time I went garbage cruising and found the crib dowels. Dad started to make a beautiful cradle that has been used by all the grandchildren and will be used by all the great and great – great ones for generations. What a visionary, none of my siblings had any kids yet and no plans to have any!

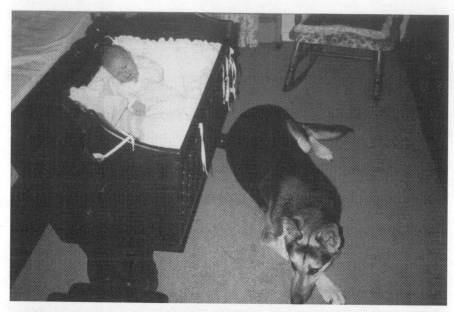

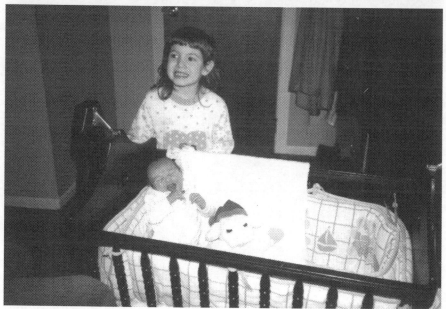

(Top) Anne with her babysitter Queenie
(Bottom) Joseph with his babysitter Anne

Poppy - Grandpa - G. Pa - Grand P

I remember that when I was young I only called my Dad, Daddy. He was "My Daddy". I love him so. I can remember back when I didn't go to school yet, that I would wait for what seemed forever for 4:00 to go to the front porch and watch for his car to come down the one way street and see where he would park. Then I would run to greet him and leap in his arms. I would always get a big hug and often a piggyback ride on his strong shoulders. One day he had a puppy in his arms and I named him Fluffy. Fluffy was never trained and barked like crazy when we had company. He would sit at the top of the stairway that led to our second floor apartment and fly down the whole flight of stairs if the bell rang. He was a great watchdog especially if someone rang the bell trying to sell us something. Fluffy would bark. Attack from the inside of the door and the person would usually just go away.

He never had an official license so one day when the inspector from the dog pound came to check, my Mom assumed that he was a salesman and ignored him. When he didn't go away, my Mom went downstairs to see who it was. As she pulled back the curtain that hung on the glass door to see better, the man held out his government id. My Mom asked what he wanted and he asked about my dog's license. At first, my Mom said, "What dog?" She was not going to get away with that one. She was really clever. By this time, the inspector had been at the other side of the door and Fluffy had been barking like a hungry wolf for several minutes. Then, my Mom said, "He's wearing it. You can come in and see for yourself." He said that he would take her word for it and left. We never saw him again.

My Dad usually remained in the background, whenever things had to be done although all major decisions were always discussed. When I got married, times were different. Every generation says that. So when my kids were young, my siblings and I discussed what our kids should call their grandparents. Grandma & Grandpa? Nanny & Gramps? Nona Anne & Grandpa Joe? We couldn't agree and it didn't matter. Our kids were going to call them whatever they felt comfortable with calling their

Grandparents. Nanny and Poppy became a regular name that was used when they were referred to as a couple. However my daughter Anne had several clever names she used, including Grand P, G Pa. I will always remember him in my heart as "Daddy".

Joseph - Chinese Restaurants - Chopsticks

When my son Joseph was young, he formed a very special bond with his Grandparents. He could be renamed Pure Love, Jr. He often waited patiently in anticipation when he knew Nanny and Poppy were coming over from Brooklyn because he knew that meant some kind of wooden toy from Poppy and some delicious food from Nanny. When both of my parents moved in with me before their condo was ready, Joseph was often glued to both of them and absorbed love from both of them. It's no surprise that from these two amazing people, Joseph's passion as a gourmet cook and incredible wood worker stemmed.

We often ate at Chinese restaurants. Even when Joseph was very little he was developing a keen eye for the potential in wood. If the restaurant had wooden chopsticks, he was very happy. If they had the cheap kind that were square at one end and fused together, you know the ones you had to pull apart and they often splintered? That was ok, they were still wood. If they had the better ones, I believe that they were bamboo, Joseph would be elated. He would ask for a set for each of us who were eating and not let us use them. He carefully put them away so that he could give them to Poppy.

My silverware drawer was often over flowing with wooden chopsticks and the second his Grandfather would come over, Joseph would run to him and give him the stack of however many chopsticks he was able to accumulate from the previous trip and say, "Grandpa, make me a toy!" That's just what my Dad did. The chopsticks were used for small toys that required small dowels to link them and sometimes were sliced for eyes on figures or headlights on vehicles! Joseph must have collected a lot of chopsticks and my Dad never threw them out. In his workshop that was passed down to Joseph there is a rather large stack of them, probably wrapped in the same rubber band that Joseph put around them over ten years ago. I know that for a fact, because they are right next to the extra roof shingles from the doll house that he made for Anne and saved, just in case.

It just dawned on me. Did Joseph love Chinese food because he loved the food or did he always want Chinese food because he wanted the chopsticks?

Garbage - Blocks of Wood - Golden Treasure

You can go to any room in my house that I currently own and find Dad's love. Forget Feng Shui to bring love and harmony; just add a little something Dad made to each room and scent it with Mom's cooking.

Where to begin with his gifts of love? My wall to wall book shelves that Dad framed with plastic molding even though I asked for oak (he thought I wouldn't know the difference); or my refinished antique piano purchased from my 90+ year old friend, Catherine, in Brooklyn, (whose relative would not include the bench because it contained old sheet music), so Dad adorned it with two refinished garage sale oak piano stools; or Dad's a.k.a. Santa's Workshop, now a shrine to him, which he tore down in Brooklyn and rebuilt in my garage?

Each one has a unique story; however one treasure was most prized by Dad, so I am much honored that he told me before he passed. When we would go shopping on our treasure hunts during the various towns' garbage pickup extravaganzas, Dad always pick up the drawers from any piece of furniture. He was most happy if the corners of the drawers were put together with dovetailed pattern and were not glued. This meant that the sides and base were real wood and not cheap plywood. It was like he had found the proverbial "pot of gold." Like a kid in a candy store, no matter how tired he was, Dad would hurry to his workshop and take unbridled pleasure in carefully separating the drawers, sizing and stack them.

Then, when the time was right and only Dad knew, the wood would be transformed into very special and one of a kind jeeps, but not just any jeeps, these were his secret legacy. The sheets were cut into specific sizes and glued together to form solid rectangular blocks. The grains in the wood would determine their position in the block. Wheels were strung together on cord. The wheels or tires for the jeep were often slices of a leg from a table we found or the side bar from an old crib. The axles were pieces of dowel, unused wooden chopsticks or leftovers from Fourth of July rockets. From that point on, most of the jeep was hand sanded or carved into the treasure. The people who drove or were passengers in the jeep were also make of wood. Dad would take a long dowel and cut slice circles into it, but not go all the way around the ¾ inch circumference. 1" then a ¼", 1" then a ¼" etc., until the dowel looked like a totem pole of body, head, body, head etc. If the wood was dark the person became a Black soldier. When he painted on the face, he would decide whether to make an Asian or Caucasian soldier. He had all nationalities covered.

The hidden secret to his Jeeps were the numbers that appeared on the hood. I learned never to assume, from Dad's jeeps. I always assumed that they were either random numbers or Dad's dog tag numbers from WWII. What may be insignificant to us could well mean everything to someone else. They were Dad's dog tag number. However, they were not in the right order for a reason. Dad didn't want his identity stolen!

Bank Trucks - Trains - Planes

Sometimes I would find something made from wood in a catalog or magazine and show Dad. "Dad, I'll buy you the pattern and the correct wood and you can make it. Would you please make it for me?" Sometimes my kids would ask him. You would think that we said something sacrilegious. Dad's motto would be, "Forget the pattern – buy wood? – they cost \$\$ – just show me." Whatever we showed him, he made and now we have many, many treasures of love.

A few, in particular, adorn the mantle and surround our fireplace. First was the train set, but not just any train set. It's the whole thing, from coal engine with real wooden coal, all the boxcars with chopstick railings and wooden beer barrel cargo to the caboose with chips of chopsticks for headlights. The detail is amazing, considering Dad often sanded the wood by hand. The wheels are awe-inspiring considering they were hand sliced from some other wooden piece. Most of our wooden treasures have the person's name inscribed so that there was no doubt that whose it was. The magnificent trains were for each of the grandchildren. Lucky me; I didn't have any kids yet at the time of the train assembly line so the train is mine! Forget the mint items that number their editions 1/1,000,000, when Dad made something and each child and each grandchild got theirs they were unique. If you were a lucky relative or very blessed dear friend you may also be a recipient of Dad's treasures. The item what you might say is, "No longer in stock and never to be made again." All Dad's work was truly one in a million.

In addition to the trains that adorn our fireplace and right next to the Army jeeps and neon green guitar, are our cherished truck banks. One for each of us with our name inscribed and best of all they came pre–loaded with money. I'm sure Mom took care of that, she was the money manager.

No entourage of vehicles in motion would be complete without air transportation. So included in these treasures is something very dear to my son. He often looked for things made of wood on purpose so that his Grandfather could make it for him. One day, in what we named the Foo Foo magazines, the items for rich people who don't know what to do with all the money they have been blessed with, Joseph's finds a wooden bi–plane. It's not just any one. It's not small. It's actually a swing for kids. How cool! So he shows my Dad the picture and asks him to buy it for him. Yeah right! Soon, when my parents visit and Dad comes in, he asks Joseph to close his eyes. Now when Dad usually came in with something reasonably sized he would just have it behind his back or in a box. So close your eyes meant that it was BIG! In came the plane! Wow, it was spectacular! Joseph was elated. Dad always made improvements to whatever he saw on paper. This plane could go on a tree as a swing and Dad made wheels so that Joseph could taxi around where ever he wanted. What a Grandpa!

And of course I can't forget the alligator pull toy that will never break because the center is a seat belt from our old Buick®.

Dialysis Angel

Trust ALWAYS that God will send the right angel just when you need it. After we lost Mom, a huge chunk of Dad went with her. His spirit for life was totally gone. His health was not great to begin with from what Dad called a good life. I guess it was the good life for people who lived through the depression and WWII. A life of doing what was necessary, when it became necessary; sharing everything with every sibling; eating whatever was put on your plate or you went hungry; working at a young age just to help put that food on the table and smoking even younger because everyone did; why not, everyone smoked, it can't hurt you even doctors smoked while they were examining you. A good adult life of healthy meat and potatoes every night for dinner, with a bag of chips each night, while you sat and watched TV for hours; weekend breakfasts of bacon and eggs and biscuits; Mom's homemade cakes and pies; Saturday late night pizza, and Sunday late night cornbread with butter and Italian pastries on Grand Street. We ate all that was good, because there were great medical doctors, who had great magic pills to solve any problem that might pop up in your body. This was a generation that trusted medical doctors with their lives and continued to do whatever they wanted to their bodies excluding exercise.

So here was Dad, at the lowest point in his life when he lost Mom and he gave up living so all his medical issues worsened. If I remember correctly, by this time in his life at age 80, he had high blood pressure and several heart attacks, open-heart bypass surgery, and the rib cage of his chest was wired together which was always interesting to see what would happen when he went through a metal detector. He suffered for as long as I can remember from dizziness every morning when he got up. It was probably a form of vertigo, something I suffered through only briefly and through the grace of God was with my chiropractor, Dr. Fred Rossi, who fixed it totally with one visit. I don't know how Dad did it for years unable to get his head off the pillow because the room was spinning so much and then very slowly while holding his head he sat up until the room stood still and then he was able to stand. Then he had a punctured eardrum, something he said was an injury from the army so he was always very fearful of getting any water in it. He never went in a pool and never went in the water when we went to the beach. His eyes were failing and were clouded even more from the rivers of tears that poured out daily for Mom. He had precancerous polyps removed from his throat when he retired. That's when he stopped smoking. His lungs were shot from the smoking and years of the daily morning ritual of coughing up pieces of them in the bathroom. The loud long hacking became my alarm. At home he often had portable oxygen to help him breathe. There were multiple bypass surgeries to remove good veins in his legs to replace bad ones or to use for his heart. His feet were numb from diabetic neuropathy. His only real fear was that they would have to amputate because they did that to his father due to the diabetes, which is so rampant in my family. My grandfather had his toes, feet and then legs amputated and spent the last years of his life totally bed ridden, totally dependent on his daughters for his very being. I know that in spite of all that was wrong with him physically, his greatest fear was that he would leave this life with amputated limbs.

It just came to me. He wanted to be a whole man so that when he was reunited with my Mother in Heaven, he would be able to run to her with the strength of his youth, like I'm sure he did when she was waiting for him when he returned from WWII. He would run and hug her as hard as he could and kiss her and dance with her and re-spark that Sunday kinda love.

In addition to all these issues, which most people would not be able to survive, Dad slowly headed toward dialysis as his kidneys failed. When he was told the horrific truth, and we learned the shocking reality of what dialysis meant, Dad refused. He said that he was ready to go and didn't want to do dialysis. Minimally, it meant another operation to put a unit under the surface of his skin, usually in the shoulder or arm, so that the dialysis machine could be hooked up to him and replace his failing kidneys. At home it would mean being tethered every night, all night, to a home unit that needed to be pumped directly to a bathroom and a spare room to store all the supplies or go to a dialysis center three times a week every week, no matter what time of year and no matter what the weather.

How do you consider the choice between the lesser evil? You do, when the alternative is dying. Even though Dad chose to die, he agreed to dialysis for my sister and me. We were not ready to lose him, not that we were when he did pass.

But Dad was still Dad, stubborn and not wanting to make a decision when it would have been a decision, and we respected that. He chose not to have elective surgery to install the unit for dialysis. Unfortunately, he waited a little too long. I remember we were eating dinner, Dad was now living with me, and he just couldn't eat a thing. I asked him what was wrong. He said, "It just won't go down." By that time the toxins had built up so badly in his body because his kidney were no longer filtering them out, that he was poisoning himself from the inside. He needed emergency surgery to put in the unit. However, because it was an emergency, they needed to put it in his neck and then later do the real surgery to implant it in his arm.

So he went for emergency surgery and began dialysis immediately. By this time in his life, my handsome, heavy Dad was emaciate and totally down trodden. He reluctantly began dialysis and went for his first session. He returned home to collapse in his recliner and stayed there until bed. Through all this, he never complained, not once. When I helped him get ready for bed and removed his shirt, it was covered in blood. Dad was drenched in his own blood and never said anything. I immediately called 911 even though he insisted not to. Our local rescue squad is amazing; they knew my house by heart. They had been there over a dozen times for Mom and now were Dad's rescuers.

It seemed they were at the door before I even turned around. They immediately assessed the situation and wanted Dad to go to the hospital. Dad refused; I don't blame him. A very young man was before my Dad and even in the chaos, Dad stopping and looked into the eyes of this very young man and asked, "How do I know you can help me. You are so young. How do you know what is best for me, someone in this situation?" The young man coyly smiled, pulled back his shirt collar and revealed his unit for dialysis attachment and said, "I know exactly what you are going through!"

The Ring - Love - Faith

My parents loved each other. I know now that they truly loved each other. Even though they fought A LOT and yelled A LOT that was the glue that cemented their love. I can remember Sundays. Mom would be slowly stirring the cauldron of meat gravy for the traditional Italian Sunday afternoon feast. She would be wearing her short sleeve dress that had snaps in the front instead of buttons and a cobbler apron whose pockets would be filled with used tissues from the post nasal drip that I realize now Mom perpetually had.

Dean Martin, Connie Francis or Al Martino records would be playing. Dad would be reading the funny paper section of the Sunday Daily News and I would be cuddled in his right arm in anticipation of what stupid thing Dagwood was going to do and Blondie's reaction. He would get up, grab Mom around the waist and give her a squeeze and swing her around and start dancing. Right there from the kitchen to the living room might well have been Fred Astaire and Ginger Rogers at the Ballroom in the Waldorf Astoria. They had that special slow and deep Sunday kinda love that's lost today in the hectic "do" and not "be" society.

Getting back to the story…when we lost Mom, Dad's simple gold wedding band ring was the only link to Mom. I can see in his teary eyes when he looked at it that the memories of those Sunday kinda love was in his heart.

Dad was always heavy, sort of a cross between Jackie Gleason, Dom DeLuise and the Godfather. Mom would give him yogurt and an apple for lunch to lose weight and he never did. He told me that he would secretly go to the lunch truck that would stop daily at the Post Office Garage where he was the supervisor, the most beloved supervisor.

When Dad got older and sick he lost so much weight that he looked like skin and bones. Lesson learned: Live the life you need to in moderation. A few years after Mom passed, Dad was so sick that he had to go on dialysis. He got so thin that his wedding ring that never came off because it couldn't move when he was heavy, disappeared one day, somewhere. He looked down at his hand to reminisce about that Sunday kinds love with my Mom and it was gone! The LAST LINK between them was gone! He was devastated.

Ever really think about finding a proverbial needle in a haystack? Think of how difficult it would be to find a ring in New Jersey? First the panic set in. I knew how important the ring was to Dad, where did we go, what did we do and who crossed our paths that day? Usually Dad stayed home on his lounge chair. But, this day, he went to a craft fair that my sister did for holiday crafts in Scotch Plains, he went to dialysis in Mountainside and we went shopping. OK, first thing were calls to each place. Then, I personally went back to each place and retraced the path we took that day. We explained to the head of the craft fair the whole situation and the importance of the simple gold band. The craft fair was at a Catholic high school and the first day school reopened, the head gathered all the kids and linked them arm in arm and they scoured every inch of the multi-acre property. They did find a wedding ring, but it wasn't Dad's. I never found out if they located the owner. The dialysis center said that even if he did lose it there, there was no way to go through the garbage because it was all covered in blood and was disposed of as medical waste. I went any way back to the center and searched every inch of the grounds, just in case he lost it walking in or out. Reliving the day was to no avail, No ring. Dad sunk to a new low and there was no bringing him out.

We had a very upbeat priest in our church and he just happened to pay my Dad a visit within the next few days. The prayerful visit centered on the ring. Father Albert assured my father that it would be found and not to worry, but how? The whole family had looked for days and kinda gave up after a week. Weeks had passed. It was Saturday and I'm not sure why since I never willingly volunteered to clean up our property, but I decided to blow the leaves off the driveway. It took a long time and I also decided to blow from the front to back rather than the back to front toward the street and sewers. Guess what? After meticulously blowing every leaf with a high powered blower, the absolute last small patch glistened a little. I could have been looking elsewhere but I was focused on really clearing all the leaves, so I was staring at the small pile. There was the ring! Dirty and dull, I scooped it up and ran to Dad. I knelt before him as he sat watching TV in his lounge chair. "What is it Boobie?" I opened my hand that had been carefully clutching the miracle. We both had a good cry and thanked God!

The Argument and the Neon Green Guitar

I know that each one of us is unique. However, if there was ever a clone of my Dad, it's my son. Perhaps my Dad's passion for wood rubbed off on Joseph since he was often at his side when Dad worked on projects in his workshop or perhaps the passion is in a gene he inherited through me because Joseph could see the potential toys in wooden chopsticks. Either way, it doesn't matter.

Joseph had a project in sixth grade to make a musical instrument. It could be anything. Most kids linked simple pipes to create an instrument to blow into; others bang on different size glass bottles filled at different levels to create music. Not Joseph, he had to make something special, it had to be made of wood, and he wanted to do it with his Grandfather. Thus, began the project of the decade, a partnership and bond between them that will last a lifetime and a series of major arguments that bonded their love for each other for eternity.

First they picked the shape. Grandpa wanted traditional, Joseph wanted electric. Decisions on what type of wood, how to cut it and sand it, what kind of strings, etc. were the sparks of their heated arguments and the glue that united them. I don't know how many of you know just how stubborn Italians can be; I believe Italian men are worse. So, when you put an 80+ year-old Italian male against a pre-teen Italian youth, you pit an immovable mountain with a tornado.

It was amazing to watch them together and more amazing that they made progress. It was very clear that even though Grandpa's recommendations were carefully considered, Joseph was in charge of the decision making for the project. They did everything together. The wood was selected and cut. It was hand sanded. Joseph wanted to buy the part that tightened the strings at the top of the guitar. Grandpa wanted to make it. So instead of spending a few dollars on a pre-made metal set, I drove them to several guitar stores. Some were very high level for professional guitarists so the sales people assumed we were buying. Grandpa just wanted to "see" what it looked like. When he was satisfied, he said to take him home and that he could make it. It didn't matter all the time and money spent on gas, we didn't spend any money on the piece. So Grandpa and Joseph drilled holed in the top of the guitar and fashioned pegs and turners by hand. They were probably made from the chopsticks Joseph gave him when he was little.

The guitar looked great, even though it was a little heavy since it was made of wood. The strings were the only part they purchased. Wooden strings just wouldn't have been right! The major decision and biggest argument was next. To Dad it was sacrilegious to paint wood. He just assumed the guitar would be stained. Joseph had other ideas; some neon color was in Joseph's mind. I can still hear the echoes of their heated disagreement coming from the shed.

I'll let you decide who won.

The next project…Dad and Joseph carefully make a knock hockey game.

Joseph went to High School, where most boys who follow the academic route wouldn't even consider taking shop; not Joseph. Sawdust must run through his veins. Here is a sample of his creations that would have made Dad very proud. Yes, he made the bench, too!

On June 8, 2010 Joseph was published and featured on the Internet on This I Believe®. Here is an excerpt from *The Family That Formed Me* that I thought you would enjoy.

"During my childhood, I grew from my grandfather's influence. He demonstrated an utmost respect for me as a child by always being patient and loving me. I was very fortunate to have someone who cared for me living in my house. He took me outside on warm summer afternoons to work in his makeshift wood workshop set up in my shed. Spending hours with a cool fan at my face and my grandfather at my side making projects such as a guitar or toy cars became the highlight of my summers. He soon changed from just a grandfather to my hero. I now realize that from him I not only learned to be patient, but gained exceptional woodworking skills. From the day I was brought home from the hospital to where I am today, I was constantly surrounded by a loving family."

Talents Beyond Wood

I realize now that everyone breaks God's mold and that each of us is uniquely unique. However, that was my Mom's favorite saying for Dad. No one will ever pass through here that is exactly like us so we better make our mark and leave a good impression. If anyone understood this it was Dad. If there was a good deed or a drop of kindness or a kind word or gentle touch that was needed, there was Dad and if he could do it without spending a penny, that was better.

If he could make something, why buy it, and if he could fix something broken, why buy a new one? He could usually fix anything and get it to work. It didn't always look the way you expected it to look. The result may have been much bigger, but it was always uniquely and perfectly a reflection of Dad.

I remember one time in particular, I had a small electrical device that stopped working. It was probably a portable radio. I gave it to Dad and asked him to work his magic. Einstein had a one-word saying over his desk that he must have learned from Dad. It was, "THINK." Dad never assumed to know it all; he just firmly believed that God gave him the common sense to figure it all out. So with any task at hand or anything to fix that he never saw before, before he touched it, he would study the situation and "THINK." There is another saying that I think Dad wrote, "Measure twice, and cut once." Dad must have mentally measured multiple times because whatever he made was perfectly done. Look once; create a treasure for generations.

So, here is Dad with an electrical gadget that won't work. Juice, that's what Dad sometimes called electricity, Juice=Motor! It must need a new motor. Now the original one fit nicely inside this portable unit. Dad fixed it all right. A short time later, Dad called me over and said that it was working fine. I remember standing there silently for a while. My broken portable radio was now blasting away, better than ever with a motor from Mom's discarded blender connected by some old and very colorful telephone wire that Dad no doubt found sitting next to it on the table. Yes it worked, but it was no longer portable.

"You can use it on your desk," he said. I'm sure being the teenager at the time, I had some sarcastic word to follow and I'm sure in Dad's infinite wisdom he didn't answer me. Little did I know then that I would give anything now just to be able to say a simple, "Thank you", and just give him a big hug and a kiss.

You Need a Lean-to

In the summer of 2002, Dad was 84. He was very frail.

He came to me and said, "You need a lean-to."
I responded, "Yeah, I'm sure I do whatever that is."

Dad always seemed to know what I needed. But, what in the world is a lean-to? Apparently, in Dad's infinite wisdom and keen eye or perhaps because every time he needed to work in the shed he tripped on or had to move our bikes, he decided that he should build an extension to the back of the shed to store them along with all the rest of the stuff that went on the deck in the summer. Knowing me, he knew that if I had an extra storage space, I would have no problem filling it.

So began the lean-to project. Since Dad was so weak, he volunteered all of us to help. Dad did what he did best — supervise, criticize and finally did most of it himself because no one ever really knew exactly the way he intended something to be.

While we were working on building it, he seemed to be in an unnecessary hurry to complete it and be exceptionally impatient. When I asked him why, he said, "I need to do it now because I won't be here next year!" Whoa, what was Dad talking about? But, he was right. He passed the next summer.

So now I have my lean-to, a monumental structure not built by an educated architect or seasoned construction worker, but by my Dad built with pure love. Yes, he also made the wagon to bring things back and forth to the lean-to.

Joseph, Dad and Jack

Dad and me

The Bird Gym

We always had some kind of pet in our home. Frogs, fish, stray cats and our beloved big shepherd, Queenie. Most were gone now and we were left with a beautiful yellow and gray cockatiel. We had two from the same birth and one had flown the coop, literally. The one that remained needed something to do. Dad and I had seen some larger birds on miniature gymnastic sets that could rival those used in the Olympics. I asked him if he could make a small gym set for our bird. With the precision of a master and I'm sure with the wooden chopsticks from Joseph, Dad created a unique gym and workout station for the bird. It even had a wooden tray at the bottom to catch any loose seeds in case the bird ate on it or to catch what might come out on the other end of the bird.

The Unfinished Perfect Fence

Even though Dad was very weak from dialysis and spent much of the rest of the time going to specialists for every other organ, he still found time and had a passion for his beloved wood. One of the last projects he was working on was a fence that would surround my Christmas tree during the holidays,

In the time he wasn't going to the many doctors, he spent much if his waking hours on a project he said I needed. He worked diligently and masterfully in his own perfection to cut, carve, and sand many exactly shaped wooden pieces that would soon develop into an heirloom fence. Once he was satisfied, the posts were placed an exact distance apart and connected by cross sections of the posts. There was even a gate. The fence was in sections so that I could make various configurations.

The fence was finished. It didn't need to be totally painted because it came from something else that was already stained. However, the tops were carved into loving peaks and needed Dad's loving touch of stain to finish them off. They never got stained. Dad was called home before it was stained. I'm often asked at Christmas time when I'm going to finish the fence. I tell the person who asks that it is perfect just the way it is.

Wooden Cars and Father Jamie

We always went to church; as far back as I can remember. It was a Sunday ritual, especially at the holidays. Somewhere between the bacon and eggs, preparing the meat gravy and going to Grand Street to see my Grandpa; there was church. I never really knew how religious Mom was until she passed and in between all the books and check books and pocket books, were the prayer cards the ones you get in the mail from all the missions and cards you get at people's funerals. Maybe because he was the only one who drove, but Dad seemed to just go to church. In his quiet, calm, mild mannered way, that's how I remember Dad's religious fervor.

There seemed to be a marked urgency to go to mass and actually talk to a priest on a regular basis after Mom was gone and more when Dad became ill. I could sense with our silent communication that he longed to speak with a priest. Often he would make the gesture in greeting, to shake hands or begin a conversation with the priest before mass and more often than not it appeared that the priest was approaching him and then appeared to go right through him as if he was invisible to greet the person behind him. Perhaps the person gave more in the collection plate. I know Dad was hurt yet he never said anything. He was a very proud man. Even when he walked with a cane to aid his failing strength he wanted to sit in the back of the church and walk independently down the center isle to receive the host.

Then one day, when I was driving him locally, he noticed that there was a new priest walking with our Monsignor Brown. I stopped the car to greet them and they responded kindly. As we pulled away, my Dad beamed. "The new priest is Italian." And so began the very brief relationship with the most invaluable priest in my father's life. Father Jamie only stayed a few months in our local parish. However, he was one of the most sincere and real priests I have ever met. He made the most lasting impression on me and most importantly on my Dad.

Father Jamie said a few masses that we attended and always greeted the parishioners with sincere love as we left the church. However, it was on July 1, 2003 that he had the most profound effect on Dad.

Dad was in the hospital and I went to stay with him for the day. Between, my sister and I we never left either of our parents alone when they were sick. It was early morning and I saw Fr. Jamie coming around the corner on the floor where my Dad's room was. He recognized me and said that he came to visit my Dad. I went with him to Dad's room, which was private. Not because we requested it but because Dad had gotten a hospital infection and needed to be separated from the other patients.

I was able to get Dad out of the hospital bed and into a chair. He seemed to have a renewed energy when he saw Fr. Jamie. They sat across from each other and I left them alone. I'm not sure what they talked about but when Fr. Jamie left, he said to me, "Your Dad said that it is ok to give me the cars." I knew what that meant. It meant he loved Fr. Jamie and that he was very, very sick. Little did Fr. Jamie or I know just how sick. It was Dad's last day and he knew it. Fr. Jamie resided over Dad's funeral with tears in his eyes and words from his heart. *I only knew Joe a very short time, from my first ever hospital visit where he met me for the first time one to one and told me that he loved me and now this is my first funeral. I will remember him forever.*

Of course I gave Fr. Jamie the last box of cars, trucks and jeeps that Dad had carefully packed up and told me I would know who to give them to. Fr. Jamie didn't give them to just anyone. He knew that they were very special. On the day Fr. Jamie left the parish I went to say goodbye. He told me then that he had finally found the right people to give them to. I don't remember all the details, but they went to a poor family who had young boys. He said that they truly loved and appreciated them. I'm glad. That's all Dad ever asked for – love and appreciation.

Wooden Cars and Father Albert

I live in a wonderful parish in New Jersey. I know that if my parents had been living in Brooklyn rather than with me when they got older, they never would have received all the blessings and love that they did from our parish priests. Father Albert was a particular favorite. A true priest since birth in Ireland, he often said that he always knew that he would be a priest. While most kids were playing house, he would play the priest residing over his family's weddings.

All the priests would come to visit my parents and Father Albert would be a special treat because he would go up to our old piano that hadn't been tuned in years and had many a stuck key and he would belt out the old Italians classics like Volare! When both of my parents started to get sick, they would get depressed and the visits from the church, from the First Friday Volunteer Angels who would bring communion and the visiting priests would really make them feel much better.

Dad rarely gave purchased gifts. However, if he really liked you, you would get one of the vehicles he made. All the First Friday Angels got one and so did Fr. Albert. He also received a few extra to give to deserving children.

I was at the church's parish center one day and noticed a little girl on the stage mesmerized while playing with something. She had the intensity of someone who had just opened the Christmas present that she really, really wanted and had to play with it. Although the center was filled, she was in her own world of make-believe. In this day and age one would venture a guess that this little girl was playing with those expensive dolls that look like you and dress like you or one of the mind numbing video games that suck all the reality of life out of you as you enter the private world of the video community. No, right there was this little girl, racing across the stage on her knees, playing with one of Dad's trucks! I was dumbfounded and very curious. I asked the little girl where she got the truck. She said that Fr. Albert gave it to her for her birthday and continued to play. Wow, I always knew my Dad's creations were made of wood now I know that that they were also made of love and that magic came through whenever and whoever played with them.

Fr. Albert had a special relationship with my Dad. He came to his funeral, but not as one of the residing priests, but as a friend. After a while, while our gashes to the soul from the loss were still fresh, I took my kids to visit Fr. Albert at his new parish. We talked and laughed and cried over stories about my parents and especially my Dad. Then, Fr. Albert confessed. He told me that he never gave the rest of the trucks away that my father had asked him to place with deserving children and that when he moved to the new parish he placed them on a shelf in the garage. He said that one day they had been knocked over. He didn't know it then, but he realized it now, the day they fell was the day Dad passed.

Mom & Dad on Momentous Occasions
Wedding — February 24, 1946

Uncle Ralph was the Best Man and Aunt Mary was the Maid of Honor

25ᵗʰ Wedding Anniversary

Lillian, Matty, and me with Mom and Dad

50ᵗʰ Wedding Anniversary

Top Row – Chris, Matty, Benjamin, Sonny,
Lillian, Marie Theresa and Jack
Bottom Row– Katie, Donna, Rebecca, Dad, Mom, Anne, Me and Joseph

Joanne Ferreri is the blessed daughter of Joseph and Anne DiGiovanna. She grew up in Brooklyn and was one of the first women selected to attend Brooklyn Poly, now NYU Polytechnic. She later received her MBA from the Lubin's School of Business at PACE University; Summa Cum Laude for both degrees. She is a member of Marquis Who's Who of American Women. After a 20 year career in corporate America with Hoffman La Roche and AT&T; she currently has her own international business with NuSkin Enterprises. In addition, she is a mentor for young adults and tutors mathematics. Joanne resides in New Jersey with her love of 35 years, her husband Jack and their two earth angels Anne and Joseph. She enjoys cooking, cycling, reading and helping others.

Dear Nancy

"Mangia Tutti"

♡ Joanne

908.581.9254

ferreri.joanne@gmail.com

THANK YOU

ALL PROCEEDS GO TO
NTC TO FEED
STARVING CHILDREN

17,000+ Meals
So far

For the Love of Food

By Anne DiGiovanna's Daughter
Joanne Ferreri

authorHOUSE®

AuthorHouse™
1663 Liberty Drive
Bloomington, IN 47403
www.authorhouse.com
Phone: 1-800-839-8640

First published by AuthorHouse 9/7/2011

ISBN: 978-1-4567-5556-0 (sc)
ISBN: 978-1-4567-5558-4 (hc)
ISBN: 978-1-4567-5557-7 (e)

Library of Congress Control Number: 2011908703

Printed in the United States of America

This book is printed on acid-free paper.

I want to publicly thank both sets of my grandparents for coming to America on what was nothing less than blind faith, exactly when they did and enduring the hardships that I can only imagine; or else I wouldn't be here right now.

However, My Mom is the real reason I'm here. I thank you Mom.

Thanks for making good decisions; first, for picking up Dad at the Rialto Movie Theater in Brooklyn. She told me she was with her girl friend and two cute guys were near them. She dropped her handkerchief on purpose to see which one would pick it up and Dad did. Next, for not sitting under the apple tree during WWII and waiting for him. Dad was away for several years and their love was though many, many letters of correspondence between them. Dad's side was from Naples, Mom's from Sicily. The forbidden love from different sides of the R.R. tracks. Mom was offered a full-length mink coat not to marry my father. I'm not sure if it was offered by her mom or mother-in-law to be. You could have had the mink coat but you chose to have Dad and then me. My grandmother on Mom's side refused to come to the wedding. At the wedding the photographer screwed up all the pictures. Luckily the milkman was there with his camera. A miscarriage before and after me, I'm here in spite of all odds. Thank you Mom, you are the best!

They say opposites attract – If Dad was the cool calm and collect one, the proverbial ICE; Mom was definitely the proverbial FIRE. Their passion for whatever they were doing was only surpassed by their love for their family. I have been truly blessed to be a part of that family. This book for my Mom could have been titled "Eat, Drink and Make Memories" because whatever she did made lasting memories in my heart and I thank you for allowing me to share some with you.

Here is the recipe for this book. The ingredients are the memories from my heart, the love I remember from my soul, seasoned liberally with Mom's passion for simply doing what was necessary regardless of what she really wanted to do, sprinkled with some secret family recipes, simmered in the zeal to always keep busy and topped off with pure love. I hope you enjoy reading it.

Table of Contents

4 Brothers - No Dad

Mom must have had a difficult life and honestly I never heard her complain about it. From what I understand, her Dad, my Grandpa Frank, worked as a Longshoreman on the docks of NYC. He was a first generation immigrant from Italy and died of pneumonia, probably caught from his job. The disease can now be cured by medicine with an antibiotic or else I wouldn't be writing this right now since I have had pneumonia several times.

Single moms have it difficult today, however I cannot imagine my Grandmother, first generation immigrant, young, no skills, language barrier, 5 kids, and to have your husband die suddenly. A single mom today may be the result of a fancy divorce or separation. The amassed fortune accumulated when two yuppies both work gets split. Then they decide how to logistically bounce the kids between parents, each of whom will invariably spoil them when they are in their charge.

Wow that must have been tough for my Grandmother. My Mom never said if her mother worked, but I do know that all her brothers did. All of them began in grocery stores and for three of the brothers; it became their life's work. My Mom began working in Clifford's Soda Shop.

Mom outside Clifford's with her oldest brother Tony.

I believe it was her first job and even though she was always smiling in the pictures, I'm sure it was tough and that most of her money went to her mother. They lived above the store on Flatbush Avenue in Brooklyn.

Mom told stories that would make my mouth water as a little kid and now brings a memory to my heart. The good old soda shop doesn't really exist anymore. A row of red topped silver stools line a sparkling clean counter with the Soda Jerk, yes that's what they called them, behind the counter to serve you. They were skilled like a top bartender in making Frappes, Malts, Banana Splits and Sodas. The Brooklyn specialty was the Egg Cream. Mom would make it for me only if I had the right ingredients. She wouldn't even consider it, unless I had U-Bet® syrup. To this day, if a store anywhere says "We Serve Real New York Egg Creams" I always ask what brand of chocolate syrup they use. If it is not U-Bet®, I walk away saying, "Fraud," under my breath and sometimes just loud enough for those around me to hear so that they will not be fooled or have a bad experience and bad mouth the famous drink of choice of New Yorkers. Mom made the best.

This was a card she sent Dad when he was in the Army.

I found these in my Grandma's treasure box. No one knows who they are. I wanted to thank them for being in my ancestry or else I wouldn't be writing this now.

My maternal grandparents Filomena and Frank Fattoruso.

I found these too. Every good Italian needs a little help.

Mom's four brothers on her wedding day: Uncle Ange,
Uncle Ralph, Uncle Sam and Uncle Tony.

Uncle Ange, Grandma Fattoruso and Uncle Ralph

Years Later – This is the only picture I have of Mom, her four brothers and Aunt Rosie. Uncle Sam, Uncle Ange, Uncle Tony, Aunt Rosie, Mom, and Uncle Ralph.

Soda Jerk - Manager - Mom

After being a Soda Jerk in her early teens, WWII began. Since most of the young men went off to war, Mom moved up to a new job. Rosie the Riveter, who became the national symbol of women who joined the work force since most of the men were gone, had nothing on my Mom. She probably could have been the national symbol and the woman who paved the way for my generation to seriously enter the work force as a professional.

Beginning as a cashier in a grocery store, Mom soon worked her way up to store manager. I could see her now going to work wearing slacks or risqué pedal pushers, pants whose length was just below the knee, probably equivalent to micro shorts worn today. Wow women's place was in the home and here was my Mom, working, jumping over counters and finally managing. She taught me that I could do anything that I wanted. I never saw my gender as a barrier to my success.

Having four brothers and being the only sister, my Mom learned early to "do" for everyone; especially iron, cook, and clean. I can't imagine the days before wrinkle free shirts, ironing a minimum of 28 men's shirts a week, as well as other clothes. At home, my Mom had laundry day when the clothes got washed and ironing night when everything got ironed. I mean EVERYTHING! I often told Mom that my underwear was just fine, but she would insist on just a light going over to take out the wrinkles in case I had an accident.

She did everything with love and passion, as if being a housewife and creating a home for her family was the greatest occupation on the planet. Silly me, I used to look down on the mundane activities of running a home. I realize now, Mom was brilliant; these activities are singularly the most important thing on the planet to do, so of course God gave the responsibility to women. It's the most important task on earth to raise a family. If the job were easy, a man would be doing it. I read a poster one time that said, "The task of raising a group of 3-5 year olds would bring most top male executives to their knees!"

It's true! Just think now of all the problems we have and how screwed up the typical American family is, with broken families, divorces, separations and the kids being tossed back and forth like tennis balls being grilled by one ex to find out with the other ex has been doing and bribed by each parent to compensate for their lack of being loving and present.

But Mom knew the secret! She really did, way before all the gurus who never had a family tell you how to raise a perfect one and way before all the child psychologists got their fancy PhDs and way before the medical doctors told you that your child has ADHD and needed drugs their whole life so that your kid grows up like a zombies and you never know their real personality. Mom knew the secret and she did it to perfection. Do you want to know it? It's love, pure and simple, unadulterated and genuine. I sensed it as a child. As I remember being very, very young and having her bathe me in the left side of the two-part

deep sink in the kitchen. The side reserved to hold the hose that drained the washing machine, which was also in the kitchen, where she filled it to mop the floors weekly. Yes the utility sink, this is where I took my bathes when I was too small to graduate to the family tub. A sink that if used today would bring neighbors reporting her to DYFS and which brings to my heart the most loving memories. Splashing in what was probably a bubble bath of dish detergent soap, being hosed down to rinse off, being lovingly laid on the kitchen table without guard rails, dried well with a small towel from Mom's hope chest, especially between the piggies and powered to probably the point of choking on the baby powder to smell good and have that just bathed feeling. All the things that are wrong today are my fondest memories.

Growing Up Italian

I was quadruply blessed, born Italian and raised in Brooklyn and having the two most loving parents anyone could ever pray for. I was told that when you are in Heaven and you are ready to be born you can pick your parents. Thank you God for helping me choose the best. We never really had a lot of money, but according to the prayer "Enough" I found neatly tucked and carefully pressed by the plastic cover of my Mom's checkbook, her sacred checkbook, we always had enough. I truly feel badly for some of today's rich kids, many who have pure wealth, anything they want at anytime, instantly, except the love, attention and time with their parents. Everyone is so busy in search of the almighty dollar that many have lost sight of what is important, the almighty family and just time together.

Some of my fondest memories of my youth are going through the Sunday ads for the local chain grocery stores like Bohack, A&P and Packers. My parents would go through each circular for the weekly specials and then with the Wisdom of Solomon and mathematical skill of Pythagoras, coordinate how much money they had to spend, what we needed, where we could get it at the best price, and what was at such a bargain that we had to get it that week.

Every Friday was the food-shopping extravaganza. We would go to each store and shop the carefully calculated "list." It was so precise that we would go to the store that had the stuff for the refrig and freezer last so that nothing would spoil. They knew of LIFO – last in first out inventory practices, without having to get an MBA.

What a team! They did everything together. My Dad would pack the groceries at the end of the check out carefully so nothing got squashed. There was nothing worse and no bigger argument than to have the super sized, enriched, no nutritional value, white bread flattened by poor packing. I often opened my lunch in the cafeteria of P.S. 269 only to find a 2" by 6" mutilated baloney sandwich and said to myself, "I guess Dad didn't pack this."

In the grocery store, my important job was to get the items on the lower shelves. My favorite was to get to select which of the giant plastic

bag of sugar coated cereal we would have that week. It was the store brand and to me at the time it was huge. I would get it and sling it over my shoulder to carry it to the shopping cart. My favorite was puffed rice because it tasted like you were having a bowl of clouds and air for breakfast. The bag was huge and cost 25¢. The cereal in a bag has been revived. However, they are on the top shelves in the store, are ¼ of the size and cost $3–$4. What a loss of memories for little kids.

Another of my executive decisions was to select the type of cupcakes to get as my treat. In the A&P there were 3 full sized iced cup cakes for 10¢. It was a no brainer. I loved the chocolate with chocolate icing and sometimes got the orange flavored with orange icing. I never got the vanilla ones because vanilla to a kid meant no flavor and was un-American. How sad, that they have discovered the wonderful fillings that I used to suck out first, is made from lard and is on the top ten foods that are most unhealthy and will kill you quicker. Today's youth doesn't know the taste they are missing.

There is one last memory of shopping with my parents. As Mom was carefully and strategically dividing and budgeting every penny, Dad was always giving me all his extras. Mom was carefully watching the checker at the checkout who had to ring up the price on every item; remember these were the days of pre-UPC numbers on every item. Every item had a stuck on price label. Dad always reached deep into his pockets and allowed me to take all his pennies to buy charms. Now for those of you who don't know what charms are, I'm sorry. You have missed out on the #1 kid pleasure of the 60's. It must have been a time prior to knowing about dirt and germs, disease and choking, because charms were tiny plastic figures with little loops on the top which were mixed with candy or gumballs in the machines at the checkout.

It was the cherry that topped off the week of school and homework – getting new charms for my collection. If you shook the machine just right and you were lucky enough, you could get the one you needed to fall into the little catcher that would be in the next pile that was dispensed with the next penny. I had a huge collection thanks to Dad and this began my obsession with collections and my love for statistics. Counting and lining up my charm collection by color, shape, etc. would keep me busy for hours!

Early Memories

*Left: All decked out for Easter – Lillian & Matty are on the top step
with neighbors Lucy & Peter Motts; Patty Pascale is holding me.
Right: Lillian and Matty are pushing me in the
carriage with my favorite Betsy Wetsy doll.*

The whole family a few years later on Easter.

*Grandma DiGiovanna with me, Lillian and my
cousins — Carolyn, Lucy and Ria.*

Our famous fig tree picture.
Our famous 719 stairs picture.
Me just having fun at 4 years old.

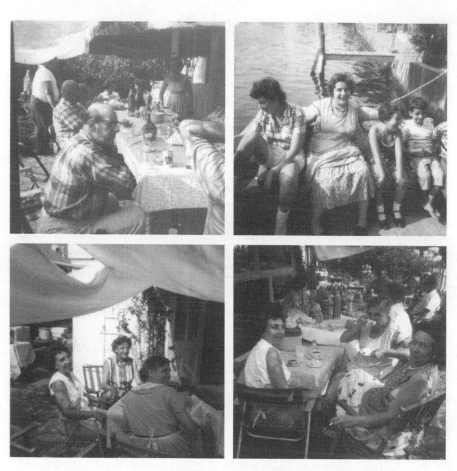

*The only picnic all the East 31st Street neighbors had with
the Pascale, Cincotta, and Salvaggio families.*

TV Babysitter and Frosted Flakes

Growing up in the 60's was incredible! It was a time like no other and it will never happen again. Who needed fancy computer games, au pairs were a fruit and foo foo designer clothing was unheard of. Give me those comfortable flammable pjs with the plastic feet built right in that would allow you to slide so far on my parent's waxed wooden floor that it could have been an Olympic sport. The ones you often had an accident in because you grew so quickly and they did not, so they were stretched so tight that it was impossible to get them off in time to pee or when you grew so quickly and since Christmas was so far off for your next pair, your mom cut the feet out and you were wearing the equivalent of spandex shorts.

However, we had a live in baby sitter. It was called the TV and not a high definition 45" wall screen with 3 remote controls and over 500 stations. Ours was black and white; yes that fact will reveal my age, with an actual on and off switch and a dial to change the channels all three of them – 2, 4, and 7. No self respecting kid would ever admit to channels 5, 9, or 11 and 13 had all that educational stuff so it didn't exist at all in a kid's mind. I was too young for public school kindergarten, and there was no need for the expensive pre-school for embryos to age 5 on every corner. However, from 9AM to noon every day, Mom knew exactly where I was and what I was doing.

My life was watching, the ritual of ½ hour sitcoms (situation comedies) that by today's immoral standard would be lame, were my life. I found each one captivating and found myself fantasizing that I was part of each family. Kids, you can go to TV Land from your cable company and watch what I am talking about except you cannot get the real effect because many have been ruined by computer digitally enhanced color.

Here are my babysitters' names: some are carryovers from the 50's and others are 60's classics. Pete and Gladys, Our Miss Brooks, Father Knows Best, Leave it to Beaver, Ossie and Harriet with Rick Nelson, Bachelor Father, Hazel, My Little Margie, Car 54, Dragnet, and I Love Lucy. I can write a book on my love for the I Love Lucy TV show and

her comic genius except I will omit my Women's Lib period where I boycotted watching it because of how Lucy was depicted as an idiot housewife under the rule of Ricky. Luckily, I came to my senses and now impress my kids by telling them the entire plot after watching less than 5 seconds of the first scene and can recite the dialog verbatim.

OK, I have to confess; I just took a 5-minute break and found a renewed love for the Internet. I Googled™ Pete and Gladys and was able to get s 5 minute clip from a 1962 episode complete with a Kellogg's® cereal commercial. Wow, the intro to the show looks suspiciously like the intro to I Love Lucy. I'm still wiping the tears away.

So why was this time of my pre 5-year old life so special? I was with my Mom. Good old Mom, I had my personal, Donna Reed, Harriet and Hazel all wrapped into one beautiful and loving woman that I could run to at any time and hug and she would invariably stop whatever she was doing and hug back! Mom always kept an eye on me, but I do wonder if she ever found out my little secret. Just in case I got hungry between my often too huge breakfast of bacon and eggs or pancakes or hot cereal and lovingly prepared lunch I hid an individual size box of Kellogg's® Frosted Flakes in the furniture.

Back Yard BBQs

I live in an upper-middle class neighborhood in a very pleasant section of New Jersey. My neighbors are all very nice and I have no complaints. Each of us has an acre of land, which is impeccably maintained on the weekend. This is the time when we wave hello to each other from our respective riding lawn mowers. Perhaps we wave hello once a month in the winter as we use our professional snow blowers. If we are lucky, we might wave as we pull out of our garages at the same time. Due to our all too busy thoroughly modern, successful duel income lives, we rarely enjoy the outdoor park that each of us have been blessed with. However, I do get a great view of the five pools that surround my property since I moved in over 15 years ago, each of which is rarely used.

What a waste of comradeship! I grew up in Brooklyn in an attached house with a 20'x20' cement backyard surrounded on three sides by two feet of soil and a shared fence with two neighbors and a church. The small strip of soil that surrounded the cement was pathetic; this became a proverbial plethora of fruit and vegetables each summer. I can see it now. In the back two corners, lived our sacred fig trees. I believe each was started from a cutting from my grandfather's trees on Grand Street. On the left was the black fig and on the right was the white one. We sometimes got black figs, rarely got white ones. Dad always said that the fruit bearing years were cyclical, I'm sure the present owners are still waiting to taste these delicacies if they haven't already cut down these trees. The young fig-trees, were developing when my young brother Matty, my sister Lillian and I were growing up. The good old days, who needed Sears to take the family holiday picture with the fake backdrop? We had the fig trees. Each year, like clockwork, dressed in our Easter Sunday best, the three of us stood in front of the fig tree for our official picture.

You would think that we had the grand ballroom at the Waldorf Astoria as our backyard. It was, compared to the small apartment over the soda shop on Flatbush Ave that housed the six Fattoruso's or the two-bedroom apartment on Grand Street that loved the eight DiGiovanna's.

It was always filled with 30 – 50 of our immediate family members for BBQs and who always did most of the cooking? Mom! Dad did get to BBQ on our 14" circular grill with recycled charcoals.

No store bought salads, no pre-packaged sauseeach, (sausages) everything was fresh! I always helped and I loved it. Whether it was peeling 5 – 10 pounds of boiled potatoes for salad or cleaning the finished basement for the parties, I loved it. The only thing that bothered me was being the youngest; I always had to run up and down two flights of stairs to get something that Mom may have forgotten to bring down, like ketchup or extra napkins. I often thought that she forgot something on purpose because my having to leave the basement to get something often coincided when Uncle Ralph came in and had a dirty joke to tell.

We're all here! If you look closely though the ever present cloud of
cigarette smoke, you will find Uncle Ralph, Aunt Phyllis and Bobby;
Uncle Tony, Aunt Rosie, Henry, Frankie and Jackie; Uncle Ange,
Aunt Vi, Tommy and Jimmy; Uncle Sam and Aunt Peewee. We
also had friends who we considered family – Nanny Carr, Ethel and
Aunt Vi's Mom and sister Mitzi with her husband Rudy. If you
could make a side dish and play cards you were always welcome.

*Just the ladies – Standing: Mom, Aunt Phyllis, Aunt Peewee,
Ethel, Nanny Carr, Rosemary, Lillian, Aunt Rosie and Jackie.
I'm next to Tootsie!*

*Years later Women's Lib kicked in and Dad let
me BBQ with Lillian and Donna.*

Leftover Macaroni - Bread and Budda - and Spaghetti on the Walls

If there was one event or fiasco that I remember vividly from when I was very young it's this one.

It seemed that Mom was always on the phone with Aunt Rosie, smoking a cigarette, reminiscing about the 40's or gossiping. Aunt Rosie would talk the most and Mom would just say "Yeah". One time I counted over 100 yeahs until she got a real word in.

My sister, brother and I would come home for lunch. One time I remember very clearly. I was in elementary school and they were probably in Jr. High and High School.

As usual, Mom was on the phone and there were a couple of pots of food on the stove. I remember Mom asking one of my siblings to feed me. Now, I'm almost sure that it was my sister because Mom never asked my brother to do anything. Since, I was young, I was not allowed by the stove, so either I asked for it or my sister just gave it to me, but I ate a buttered roll, which was probably being saved for dinner or my Dad's lunch.

Somewhere in this time frame my Mom got off the phone. I don't know if she told my sister or she just assumed that my sister would know, but I was supposed to be given the left over spaghetti and meatballs for lunch. Often if there was left over macaroni from the traditional Sunday gravy and Thursday leftover gravy diners, we got a special treat and had it fried for lunch.

That was the deal on this occasion; however there must have been some miscommunication. When my Mom stepped into the kitchen, it was instant WWIII. You would have thought that someone was lying dead on the ground! There was instant screaming and yelling and a dumbfounded look on our faces as we sat around the table eating so that we could all get back to our respective schools within the hour. "What's going on in here? Why didn't you eat the leftovers? Why did you eat the rolls? *!*!"

Then, like a surreal event, you know the kind that is happening right

in front of you and you can't believe it, Mom picked up the pot of spaghetti and threw it all over the place. Now this might have been a noble gesture to a pre-punishment lesson for disobeying had it been a weekend, but all of us had to go back to school, so Mom would have to clean up. This was no ordinary clean up punishment like we used to get – "Go clean your room" and instead we would go listen to records for an hour. This was thick red tomato sauce, meatballs and 12" long spaghetti. This scene was probably where the saying, "Throw the spaghetti on the wall and see what sticks," originated. So after what seemed like an eternity, but really lasted only five minutes of yelling, smacking, threatening; I took off for school crying my eyes out. It was years later that I found out that Lillian didn't go to school that afternoon and just sat on the porch paralyzed to go and too afraid to go back in the house to help. I'm not sure what happened to my brother. Knowing him, he probably just shrugged his shoulders and shook his head believing none of this was his fault or his responsibility.

Lunch at Irene's with Mom

I'm sure that Mom felt guilty that I had to spend my lunch hour in the back of a store. I hope that deep in her heart she believed those lunches were some of my best memories. Mom had a part time job around the corner from our house to make extra money and as she put it, "to make ends meet." I didn't know what "making ends meet" really meant, but I have a good idea growing up and living with the masters. The first priority was always *us kids*. Everything was simpler then. We each got two new outfits when school started, a new pair of shoes, and a new briefcase for elementary school or book strap if we were older; one Easter suit with a hat; and at Christmas our one present we wanted sprinkled with a lot of chotchkies (these are the little junk toys and goodies that we all love, don't need, and discard or give away within the year.) About a year ago I found my brother's briefcase loaded with worksheets and research papers and he is retired! I sent it to his daughter because I'm sure he would have immediately thrown it away. Oh, the things we mothers deem as invaluable. I wonder what my children are going to do with the left over umbilical cord I saved from each of their births?

The next thing that the masters of "making ends meet" did was *to always have food in the house* and *an incredible hot meal on the table promptly each day at 4:45 PM.* My parents could have opened our front door and hung the proverbial shingle out – **Grocery Store.** The refrigerator was always filled with first times, leftovers and indisputable weekly bargains from each of the grocery stores. Mom always made extra just in case. One time, my Mom negotiated a really cheap price for a case of persimmons that most people would have considered ready for the garbage, not Mom, see knew the secret. If you were lucky enough to catch them just at the right consistency somewhere before mushada (mushy) and ducada (ready for the garbage) you would have a delicacy that is difficult to surpass. Mom hit this one right on the head. She carefully carried these treasures separately in their treasure chest, which was the bottom from the cardboard soda case and headed home. We had a feast that night.

The treasures in the refrigerator were only equaled to what was

stocked in our pantry. Now by most of today's standard of room size, walk in pantries ours would have been considered miniscule, but not to me. It was an adventure! Actually, it was a refurbished dumb waiter. Now for those of you who don't know what that is, a dumb waiter is like a food elevator, delivering goodies between floors. Our house was a simple two family attached house so the reason why there was even a dumb waiter was always a mystery to me, but it made our house special. Since we had no need to pass food between our tenants and us, Dad closed off the dumb waiter, built a base and made it our pantry.

He was the stock boy. Everything had its place: Campbell's® soup in the lower left, canned vegetables to their right, all sorted by type then sized and all facing front. Dad was a stickler for putting things in their proper order and having one place for everything. He always said, "You can borrow anything I have as long as you put it back where you found it."

So the "making ends meet" experts had the kids and food covered; smother that with unconditional love, what else does a person need? Nothing, absolutely nothing! I rarely saw my parents buy anything for themselves and when they did get something for their birthdays or Christmas, it usually stayed in the plastic wrap in case it needed to be returned.

It just dawned on me, the trouble with children in today's society is that "unconditional love" has been replaced by "unconditional things"– iPods, Wiis, homes so big no one sees each other, computers, trips to exotic places alone, gift showering, alternating weekends with divorced parents, etc. I could fill a book with this list alone. Society, listen! Get back to basics – love first, be present, listen to each other with your heart twice as much with your two ears and you will have to reprimand only half as much as you speak with your one mouth. Hug often with your two arms – tell everyone you love them (even if it is to yourself in the silence of your heart) it will melt even the hardest head – tell everyone they are your Best Friend. I learned this from my son who told me, "Who said you can only have one best friend?" We have two eyes, ears and arms, one mouth and an infinitely large heart. I learned this from my first born when I gave Anne my entire heart and then realized I was also able to give Joseph my entire heart whenever and wherever it was needed. God got the proportions right, we just have to use them.

Back to my lunch at Irene's story. During my lunches at Irene's, I always ate in the back cubby hole where everything that couldn't be squeezed into the cluttered store ended up. Eating "heads up" would be an understatement. At any time, boxes, bras or body parts from decapitated mannequins could come flying at me. Thank God these were the good old days before the OSHA standards for construction and employee safety. The bathroom, also used for storage, was lit by a single bulb, which was turned on by a pull chain that I couldn't reach; so if I needed to use the bathroom I had to call my mother. Mom would be working. She would check on me constantly to make sure that even if I got hit by some inventory, I was still ok. In those days, there weren't any prepackaged, precut, neatly wrapped in plastic, perfectly proportioned lunch for a child. I got a sangwhich (yes, I meant sangwhich that's how you pronounce it correctly in Brooklyn) on white bread – none of that nasty healthy stuff. My favorite was Trunz baloney on soft white bread with mustard, the stuff that clogged arteries are made of. Who knew? Who cared? Back then when you got old you just had hardening of the arteries and used those exact terms as you ate bread and budda and washed it down with soder, then had a cuppa coffee with a cannoli and a cigarette. Aaaah, the good old days!

Not too long ago, I drove past my old house and made a left off East 31 and believe it or not, there on the corner of Glenwood Road and Avenue H was Irene's! It may have had a different name, but it was unmistakably Irene's. Still there with the horribly scary female mannequins from the 40's whose heads could be twisted and whose arms fell off and whose eyes you'd swear followed you while you shopped to catch you shop lifting!

Scrabble Afternoons

Mom was brilliant. I was the type of kid that had to be kept busy…very busy. If I were growing up today, the doctors might suggest medicine to calm me down; Mom just kept me busy, not with meaningless activities, but with trips to the library as often as necessary and workbooks that she disguised as fun books. I was always reading, always doing something to keep myself busy. My goal was to read all the books in the library. Ambitious? Not for me. My Mom or older siblings would read to me before bed when I couldn't read yet. When I learned to read before kindergarten thanks to them, I could go through a couple of kids' books a day and by junior high I was reading the "without pictures" books in a few days. My insatiable energy was tamed between reading books and doing all the math workbooks that you could buy at the local drug store. In kindergarten I was given some special placement test in the basement of PS 269. I still remember taking it, placing color blocks in correct holes and answering questions in an atmosphere that resembled the Nazi interrogation. That test, when I was 5, determined that I would spend the next 12 years in accelerated classes destined for college. By 6th grade, I was reading at the 12th grade level. I won many awards upon my graduation from 6th Grade. However, I was unable to attend the awards ceremony because it was on the same evening and at the same time as my band concert that I couldn't miss because I was 1st clarinetist! So Mom and Dad went to receive my award and got to school just in time to hear me play in the concert. I went on to graduate with honors and be one of the first women admitted into Brooklyn Poly with a math scholarship. Poly has recently become NYU Polytechnic. After completing my undergraduate degree, I was the only person in my family to go on to graduate school, let alone get straight "A"s in my MBA.

I say none of this to brag, instead to tell you that if your child can't sit still to reconsider giving them Ritalin or some sedatives and to take the time to find their passion. I owe all my success to my Mom who constantly encouraged me. She had a warm meal waiting for me when I got home from school every day – even through graduate school to get

my MBA. She used to tell me to go do my homework after I cleared the table, just like when I was 5, even though I was in my 20's. She washed my clothes the second I took them off and didn't rearrange my books when I was studying especially for finals – THANKS MOM. I owe all my success to you!

I especially remember our Scrabble® afternoons. Mom, in her quiet internal and eternal brilliance led me away from after school cartoons and towards our Scrabble afternoons. I would come home daily to a Scrabble board set up. I'm not sure if she let me win to boost my confidence, however I usually did win. I loved playing with her. At first we would be serious and be in competition to win. Then, if I got stuck she would help me or let me check in the dictionary to see if a word I wanted to use was real. I learned recently that this maneuver is called a head fake in football; you look or do something in one direction and really go in the other. I'm sure that my Mom never knew she was doing a head fake on me by allowing me to learn and play by the rules of Scrabble®. I learned to negotiate with cross team players, strategize to win and congratulate the winner if it wasn't me. I could go on and on with the life lessons I learned however at the time we were just immersed in our Scrabble® afternoons.

I try to keep a similar time now with my daughter just for us. We call it "girl time". It must have worked because Anne always sends me a note or calls me right before she comes home on a visit from college and says, "Mom, don't forget about our girl time." Our best and most memorable "girl time" that will go down in the history of "girl time" was the few precious days we spent together at Walt Disney World Resort in Orlando, Florida in May 2008, when I picked her up from her semester of working at Disney's Contemporary Resort. She may never know just how proud I was of her being selected as one of only five people from UMASS Amherst for the program that semester. She may never know the life lessons I learned from her over those few days as we head faked it being our respective birthdays and got magical treatment in every park! I'm still working off the 6 free Mickey shaped ice creams.

On my Scrabble® afternoons with my Mom, I recall a play that I was able to make during one game that should go down in the Scrabble® Hall of Fame. On the Scrabble® board there are 8 invaluable spaces that any player would know is worth the most points. It's the precious red triple word spaces. One day I played the word of a lifetime. I had a 7-letter word

33

that crossed 2 triple word squares, I used all my tiles and had a double letter square included. I don't remember my exact score, but I must have had some high value tiles in the word because I remember the value being over 60 points. Probably the most valuable lesson I learned was to be humble because once I achieved the "2 triple word, double letter, using all tiles" title, Mom knew that she might never win again. She was humble and I played daily, not to beat her but to beat my previous day's score. To compare yourself to others is not good, to improve over your self is everything. I'm not sure if Mom realized just how important these Scrabble® afternoons were to my intellectual growth, individual pride, and team spirit. I didn't know then, but now I do – THANKS MOM.

Somehow our finishing the game was always perfectly timed and coincided with Dad coming home for dinner. Every day I would share with him how much I beat Mom by and she wouldn't say a word. What more could a kid ask for?

One Christmas I graduated from the cardboard Scrabble® set with missing letters to the best Christmas present, a plastic deluxe Scrabble® set, the one with the edged spaces and peg scoring capability which I still can't figure out. I still have both boards and play with my kids.

Unforgettable Birthdays

Kids today get designer everything, hundreds of dollars, and trips to exotic places for their birthday. I didn't get any of those things. However, my birthdays were very special because of my Mom.

She would invariably wake me up with a kiss and a balloon, which to this day I don't know where Mom pulled it out from. She couldn't have hid it in the corner of her bedroom where she hid everything, so this balloon was magic. A balloon and a kiss was all I really needed, but Mom made the whole day special. My gifts would be wrapped with perfection and arrive with the balloon. Since Dad was at work and my brother and sister were already at school, it was a mixed blessing to see these lovingly wrapped treasures because I would have to wait all day in anticipation of what was in them until after dinner when we had cake.

If my birthday fell on a school day, my Mom would surprise me during snack time with a tray of homemade cup cakes for my entire class. No store machine-made, untouched by man cupcakes, just ones made with love by Mom, delivered by Mom as a surprise even though I knew she would be coming. I would relinquish my favorite chocolate cupcakes for vanilla or a mix of both because some kids might have been allergic to chocolate. Ah, the good old days. Chocolate allergy was the only one I had ever known growing up; chocolate and being allergic to your brother's cooties. Today the allergies run the gamut of nuts, flavorings, spices, gluten, lactose, flowers, and air. The future is going to remember us as the label generation, who had to read every label for ingredients, or the bubble generation who should have been placed in a germ free environment. I grew up without labels on food where the fat Campbell® Soup Kids Chicken Noodle Soup was my cold medicine and I would run and jump into a pile of fresh raked leaves in the fall! So, here I was at snack time, beaming because my Mom brought cup cakes and I was blessed with another round of Happy Birthday. If snack time was right before going home, I would have the extra bonus to walk home with her.

After school, a special snack would be waiting for me and of course the presents that I couldn't open yet, then came dinner. Wow! No fancy

restaurant. Mom would make me whatever I wanted. I don't think that I intended to give her so much extra to do, I just loved this meal and it took a lot of time. I love stuffed squid over spaghetti.

Back in those days, calamari didn't come cleaned and washed. It only came in a massive 5 pound frozen block of unclean, heads (tentacles) on squid. Mom would have to defrost it without the aid of a microwave, careful not to let the liquid spill because it stunk up the house for a week. Once separated, the transparent outer skin would have to be removed. The tentacle head had to be very carefully separated from the body or the purple squid ink from the eyes would shoot out. I remember ducking and yes not ducking in time when I helped. Forget the Tide to Go® stick. Nothing would help remove the dye stain.

Now, squid comes defrosted and cleaned. I don't know if you have any idea what is inside the body cavity of a squid. You have to reach in and pull out what can only be described as a 2"or 3" long by ½"-1" piece of solid translucent pointy tipped bladed edged plastic. Yuck!

The beak had to be removed carefully from the head or if you were unfortunate to have it in your mouth when you took a bite at dinner you would invariably spit everything out and say, "What the hell was in that piece of Galamaaad?" Galamaaad – that's how true Italians pronounce calamari. After the squid was cleaned it was washed, carefully washed and lovingly filled with a secret bread crumb mix and then it became part of a delicious secret tomato sauce that went over my spaghetti. The process to create this meal was gross; however, Mom never complained and made it just for me for my birthday dinner.

Then the cake was served. Whatever I wanted and I always wanted chocolate cake with chocolate pudding filling and chocolate icing. It went on the plate that spinned and played Happy Birthday with the used birthday candles on top from my last or someone else's cake that were only on for the minute you sang the most often sung song in the world – Happy Birthday. The extra perk was the yearly appearance of my 4" thick personalized birthday candle that I got from Elly Pascale when I was born which burned down ¼ " to mark exactly how old I was until I was 21.

Finally, my presents could be opened. It didn't matter what they were; they were just all mine. My Mom would tuck me into bed and kiss me. My balloon would blow, tied on my bedpost and I would close my

eyes in complete comfort, joy, and satisfaction at the end of my perfect birthday.

I do my best to recreate what I can for my kids to someday have memories like mine of a perfect birthday. We may have pizza for dinner. I still make their cake and they have their own personalized candle but it's just not the same without Mom.

Matty, me and Lillian on my 20th birthday.

To Trick or Treat or Not to Trick or Treat

Just when I thought I was finished with every story that I had in my heart, one surfaced that must be added. This is a story of what never to do to your child. Mom I love you and Mom I have long since forgiven you, but the awful truth must come out. Today is October 31, 2008, that is to say, Halloween and a memory that I had long since buried resurfaced and sent chills through me.

Since I was always bigger than all the kids, you know the last one on line in school and the kid who always got to sit in the back of the room, my Halloween Trick or Treat days were limited.

Mom would say, "You are too big to go Trick or Treating."
I would reply, "Mom, I am still in elementary school!"
"You are still too big", she would say.

Luckily, I correlated being big with having more brains and being smart so I always got "A"s. Being big was my mixed blessing that I have had my whole life. Being Catholic has always been a blessing, however, being Catholic on Halloween in the 70's as a kid I questioned one rule. I never really understood this one but Mom assured me it is in the official Catholic Rule Book. "Thou Shalt not Trick or Treat on Halloween if it falls on a Sunday!" Please write it down if you never heard it before.

So what do you think happened one Halloween? What an evil trick. It's worse than being born on Friday the 13th, so that there is always a little extra of the devil in you. Worse than having your birthday fall on February 29 so you are ¼ of your real age and you don't really know what that is. Worse than having your birthday fall near Christmas so they just split in two what you would have gotten for Christmas. One year Halloween fell on a Sunday and no matter how hard I begged, Mom reminded me of the rule and she wouldn't give in. Since I was only 9 or 10 years old, a little shy of 5'6" and still in elementary school, what's a girl to do? This may be the last year that I can go Trick or Treating before I reach the official "you are too big to go" height limit. I went trick or

treating on Saturday, October 30 all by myself, all dressed up, a day early and embarrassed beyond anyone's comprehension.

Imagine this scene: a chunky...ok fat little kid, too tall for her chronological age, dressed in some made up indistinguishable costume because I threw it together like I did every year from whatever I found in my closet, and wearing a full length winter coat over my costume. I go door to door ringing bells saying, "Trick or Treat" a day early. Here are some of the remarks I remember and that I can write for any reader, "What are you an idiot?" "Halloween is tomorrow." "Go away." "Don't you know what day it is?" Some people were kind enough to open their door. I explained my situation. Some slammed the door in my face; others took pity and gave me candy as long as I promised not to come again the next day for seconds. I vividly recall ringing the doorbells of a section of two family homes and having someone open their window on the second floor. Our conversation went something like this:

"What do you want?"
"Trick or Treat?"
"Halloween is tomorrow?"
"I know. I'm Catholic and can't Trick or Treat on Sunday."
"Go away."
Then they took pity on me. I must have looked very pathetic.
"No, wait. I'll get you some candy."

So they went away for a minute and returned and threw some candy at me. I closed my eyes and ducked not to be hit and had to pick up what I could find from the sidewalk and dirt. After my fun Halloween Eve day, I returned home. Not with the big bag of stuff that I usually got, but with a few pieces of candy and some fruit that went right in the garbage because in the 70's fruit on Halloween had razor blades in them. How horrible for those forward thinking health conscious few who wanted to give out a healthy treat. So let me end my memories of a past Halloween here.

Unless you grew up Italian in Brooklyn, you may find the following stories difficult to believe, but I assure you they are true! Holidays were what we lived for, almost like the mass calendar and schedule, anything between New Years, Easter, Thanksgiving, and Christmas was just "ordinary time."

Each holiday had its special and unique foods that you could only have at that holiday. My childhood was made up of traditions. Today kids get whatever they want whenever they want it. Winter watermelon! Summer pumpkins! AHHH! What a shame, nothing is really special. Some of my best childhood memories are that of holidays and the associated foods for each. Each holiday meant a special mass surrounded by holiday food. Mom was a genius, linking mass with food. Both became passions in my life.

Easter meant a bizza gran – grain pie. There was also a bizza rustica – meat pie, but too often the Prosciutto de Parma was too much money. So mom stuck with the grain pie. I have to be honest. I really didn't like it because of the cubed citrus fruit that was used. I enjoyed the wheat crunchiness and the ricotta, it was like a soufflé dessert but the citrus was hard and gooey. Mom would always save some of the wheat, cook it and we would have it for breakfast with milk and honey. The round grains were supposed to symbolize Saint Lucy's eyes, so eating the grain during Easter meant that your vision would improve. I firmly believed this.

The true mark of my Mom's improvising any existing recipe was the fact that she never measured the liquor. Even if the recipe didn't call for liquor Mom would always add a shot or two, just for flavor. No wonder my fruit salad isn't as good as hers, I forgot the Sambuca®! When Mom made the pies, she didn't just make one for us to share. She made one for each brother, one just for Dad, some for friends, some just in case, and a large one for the holiday dinner table, after we were all stuffed. Since we didn't have a dining room table, I knew the holiday was near when her bed was filled with pies!

Thanksgiving was the traditional lasagna, followed by the turkey

dinner extraordinaire and homemade pies. I don't believe store bought or readymade was in Mom's vocabulary. Lucky for me, I got the real stuff, all made with pure love.

Christmas, now that was the biggest feast because it lasted two days and there was no time for digesting any of the previous meals because you just ate continuously. While you were waiting for the meals, you picked. When I was little, Christmas Eve was at one of my Dad's sisters. On Grand Street we would be at Aunt Fay's and Uncle Charlie's to eat and would run up and down the six-family attached house to Aunt Josie's and Uncle Danny's with Bootsie their dog hot on our trail. Each aunt would decorate their living room with what seemed to me as a little kid like an endless snow covered magical Christmas village. The entire length of each of their living rooms was covered in pristine white sheets of authentic cotton snow. The numerous village homes were lit up and the people in the village were each specially placed with loving care. There was even a circular skating rink of carefully cut aluminum foil for the ice. I remember vigilantly looking at each of my aunt's works of love in total unadulterated amazement for a long time.

Sometimes, we would go to my Aunt Mary's and Uncle Adrian's. I remember one special Christmas Eve that their white German Sheppard had puppies. I can visualize the corner of the kitchen gated off filled with puppies, all wearing red bows and the joy in my heart when I was allowed to pick one up. All the kids from my Dad's side were at Aunt Mary's. Now since Dad had two brothers and 3 sisters and each had at least 2 kids and many of my cousins were older and had two to four kids themselves, I could never understand how all of us would invariably miss Santa's entrance. However, it was OK since he always left a huge, over six feet, sack of goodies for the kids.

My Uncle Adrian would make his famous fish salad. There would be roasted sausage from Grand Street and the infamous disgusting liver incased in a fatty sheath. We were forced to eat one piece on Christmas Eve probably on a gesture of being healthy among the Italian pastries of cannolis and sfogliatelle. It was gross. I can recall pulling out the whole piece of fatty covering from the back of my throat because I just tried to swallow it without chewing. Needless to say, I never touched this food again. When I was older, we spent Christmas Eve at my Uncle Ange's and Aunt Vi's. She made the best pound cake with a dozen eggs and a

pound of butter. Years later, we went to Uncle Ange's and Aunt Lee's for the best new traditional Christmas Eve of Jewish potato knishes!

Christmas day came after a night of feasting on carbs and sugar. I really don't remember how long my Mom used to cook, it was so long it became a blur, but everyone on Mom's side came to our house, which didn't have a dining room. The living room couch went into their bedroom and our living room was transformed into a restaurant of irregular folding tables with weak side flaps that always gave way when you leaned on them, discarded bingo tables from the Jewish Temple across the street and a kid card table. It was a big deal to graduate from the kid table to the adult table. It was sort of an Italian Bar/Bat Mitzvah when you were initiated into adulthood. The cacophony table parade extended into my parent's bedroom and their bed served as the dessert buffet table. On Christmas, Mom made tons (no exaggeration) of cookies; my favorites were the ones from the cookie gun – butter, cream cheese, and spritz cookies. Whatever a spritz is, they were delicious. They were my favorite because I got to help her when she made them. The table was filled with assorted jellies and nonpareils, sprinkles and homemade icing to decorate the cookies. My favorite dessert by far was Mom's secret recipe struffolis! It was a secret recipe because she didn't follow one and just mixed stuff until it was right. Cut the dough into tiny balls then fried them and they swelled into ½" thick treasures that took a bath in honey, nuts, and sprinkles.

On Christmas day everyone was there, all the aunts, uncles, and cousins on my Mom's side. Oh, by the way, "sides" never mixed except at weddings or funerals because they had to. Invariably, sometime between 1930 and 1980 someone made a remark that no one could quite remember but someone was always not talking to someone else. I didn't even know that I had four uncles until I was over 13 years old. I thought maybe we adopted them at that time.

Anyway, we never let arguments get in the way of food. Christmas was a real feast that would make King Henry weep. Suddenly, money became no object. We would start with antipasto, only the good stuff, homemade, Boars Head® and imported Prosciutto de Palma not Prosciutto de Brooklyn, the salami was rolled as tight as toothpicks, the imported and specialty cheeses were abundant; the provolone was so sharp you could cut your tongue on the edges, the thought of the Polly-O® basket cheese

is making my mouth water as well as the fresh roasted red peppers, black olives, and celery in pure extra virgin olive oil salad. Mom always got the colossal pitted black olives, which I would put on each of my fingers and pretend that they were fairytale characters. Who needed to buy finger puppets? Each character looked exactly the same so that I really had to use my imagination and when I was bored with my new finger puppet toy, I just ate them!

Next came the soup. I inherited my Mom's soup cauldron, the official chicken soup maker, although I rarely use it because it is so big. I will always keep it because it is a treasure. However, I still wonder if the chips off the enamel could potentially contain cadmium, a toxic substance that could lead to poisoning. When I was growing up, no one even thought of being poisoned, your mom would probably just wash your mouth out with soap. Mom's chicken soup was the best and to date hasn't been duplicated. It was loaded with vegetables, but she would strain them by hand through the schoolabasta (macaroni strainer) and shred the chicken so that you were left with the richest and most delicious broth. She would then make ajanee babe (Acini Di Pepe) and fill the dish with these tiny soup macaroni and smother them with the rich broth. She would also make a special sweet extra thick tomato sauce using only paste. Dad wouldn't eat her soup unless she made the sauce. A dollop of sauce would be stirred in and then a smothered with Pecorino Romano grating cheese. If we were extra lucky and Mom made the soup with the family size package of chicken necks, she would take the boiled necks out of the soup and cover them in minced garlic and broil them until they were crispy and we would dip them in the special extra thick sweet sauce. Yum! After the soup, came a light pasta dish of homemade lasagna, stuffed shells, ravioli or cannelloni with meat sauce. Meat sauce for the holiday included – meat balls with raisins and pignolis, sausages – both sweet and hot, pig skin if we were lucky, neck bones and brajol (beef braciole) – a magical mix of onion, pork fat, raisins, pignoli and hard boiled eggs all lovingly enrobed in the thinnest pancake of lean beef.

The real meal came after these appetizers. There was always some kind of meat and when we couldn't decide, Mom made two – turkey, ham, pork roast or an occasional leg of lamb. Around the meat would be platters of fresh potatoes sweet and regular roasted or whipped with cheese or marshmallows, 5-10 pounds of giant stuffed mushrooms,

stuffed artichokes, and cold steamed broccoli with lots of garlic and fresh lemon.

About an hour later after we finished eating, when we had digested, the tables got efficiently cleaned with the cooperative effort of all the women. It looked like a fire bucket brigade of dishes being handed off, leftovers being wrapped to take home, and someone washing, and someone drying. There was no dishwasher then, just Aunt Rosie. Tootsie would be taking the coffee count regular or black and Mom would be hunting for the Italian espresso pots that you turned upside down to make the coffee. The men just stayed out of the way of the hurricane of activity. In less than half an hour, out came the desserts – direct from the bed buffet. In addition, there were pounds of roasted nuts and Grandpa's nutcracker that looked like a hallowed out 4" slice of a tree with a metal center and mallet to break the nuts with. There were figs on a string, finookie (Finocchi or fennel), and thin mints.

New Year's Eve was primarily appetizers because everyone was still full from Christmas. Don't get me wrong, we had tons of cool appetizers. Everyone got a glass of champagne at midnight and the New Year's celebration was lead by Guy Lombardo. It was so important to watch Guy Lombardo that I really believed that when he died, there would no longer be a New Year. I'm going to share with you a little known secret to success. On New Year's Eve, exactly at the stroke of midnight, you have to have money in one hand and be eating creamed herring!

Traditions have become a lost art. I'm so grateful to have been able to experience so many delicious ones. Thank you, Mom and Dad!

I was about 1½ years old this Christmas. Wasn't I adorable?

*Christmas Eve at Aunt Mary's and Uncle Adrian's basement with the
player piano and liver after midnight mass. Fond memories, I wouldn't
have it any other way. Lower left – my cousin Kathy hid Dad's pants. He
laughed along with us. The picture in the upper left hand is of my cousin
Matty and my proud Grandparents when he made his Confirmation.*

First Christmas in my Fanwood home. Mom and Dad sitting, Sonny, Jack, Lillian holding Marie Theresa, Me, Matty holding Chris and Donna holding Katie.

Christmas in Mom and Dad's new Brooklyn home. Dad is holding
Katie, Mom is holding Anne, Marie Theresa and Chris are sitting.
Jack and I; Donna and Matty & Lillian and Sonny are standing.
The feast is cooking.

Here we are creating new holiday memories for my kids.
Mom, Dad and Donna prepare spadinis. Notice the mallet
in Dad's hand? Yes, that's the mallet he made as a young
boy on Grand Street for his Mom – What a treasure!

Mom and Aunt Lee nosh while Uncle Ange carves.

First Christmas in our Millington home. Marie Theresa is in front with Lillian and Sonny; Dad is holding Joseph; I'm holding Anne; Mom and Jack. Thank you Lillian for making the great matching Christmas tops!

Regrets

"Regrets, I have a few but then again too few to mention," is a line from a famous song. I have held a few regrets in my heart and I would love to share them with you since they have recently resurfaced as they often do. They may seem very small, even inconsequential; however, I have held them in the core of my soul for so long that I believe if I get them off my chest I can go on completely cleansed from any remorse.

The first was when I was very young; I couldn't have been more than 4 or 5, my Mom was going to buy pizza. Some of my fondest memories are visions of my mother turning the corner of Glenwood Road and East 31Street with a pizza box in her hand. Now living in Brooklyn meant that practically every other store was a pizzeria, they were the Starbucks® of the 60's. However, not every pizzeria was created equal. There was the basic neighborhood pizzeria where they were never too crowded so you could drop in any time for a slice of abeetz (Italian for a pizza). Then there were the pizzerias that had "specials." My Mom worked in Irene's Lingerie, a woman's clothing shop around the corner, and on certain week nights, a whole pie, are you sitting, was only $1.25! Saturday evening, during the commercials of the official Saturday night family movie, Mom would often start the chant, "pizza, pizza" and our mouths would salivate. She would get up and buy a pizza as our snack. It just came to me, no wonder I have a pizza addiction and consider myself a pizza aficionado.

Now there are 8 slices in a pie and 5 of us. Being the math genius, it was a no brainer. We would each have a slice and equally split the remaining 3 slices – we would each get 3/5ths to be precise. NO, not in an Italian family, that had a husband and Italian husband in training, i.e. my brother. They each had a FULL extra slice; if we were lucky and my Dad or brother didn't want the last slice, my sister and I could share it. My Mom always said she was full. How unfair to the backbone of our family, the most loving, kind, and giving person on the earth, my Mom. She was never even considered for the last slice.

By the way, the Italian lion rule, i.e. males eat first and all they want first was required not only for pizza but pork chops, meat loaf and the other of Mom's delicacies as well. They also got to taste a sacrificial virginal (no sauce) single macaroni that was specially selected from the pot of boiling water on Sunday, to see if it was done. God forbid a woman wanted her macaroni al dente and her man wanted them mushy – she would lose hands down, ALWAYS. I hope my husband doesn't read this.

Now, there was one very special pizza place, Lenny's, you would have to walk about 4-5 long Brooklyn blocks to get there and since Mom never drove she walked there. Lenny's was the "official" Friday pizza place. When I was growing up in a good Catholic family in Brooklyn, you were forbidden to eat meat on Friday! I'm not sure when Jesus changed the rules or when he made them in the first place, but when I was growing up, you would have to go to confession or Hell if you ate meat. I remember if by accident meat touched my mouth because I didn't know that meat was in the food, ahhhhh! I was going to Hell! One time I ordered spicy eggplant at a Chinese restaurant that had ground chop meat in it and another time, I completely forgot that it was Friday and took a bite of a burger. I 911ed the church and ran to confession.

Back to my Mom's Lenny's story. Lenny's was just a neighborhood pizzeria, however, if there was ever the mother of all neighborhood pizzerias and the only one that any self-respecting Italian Catholic would get their "official" Friday dinner from, it was Lenny's. Wow, it just dawned on me. No meat on Friday was not started by Jesus, it was started by Italian house wives. They needed a one night break from cooking humongous meals and having to have them hot and ready on the table at any time their husband decided to sit down armed with a knife and fork in his hands. I'm not kidding. Dad would sit at the table each night with a knife in one hand and a fork in another perfectly perpendicular to the table and say, "Where's dinner?" It didn't matter what it was, it just had to be ready. I must say that my Dad did this act lovingly. I've witnessed my friends' fathers sit in the same position at their respective kitchen tables and pound on them with all the ogreness of Shrek! I can't be judgmental; it's just what that generation did. Thank God my husband doesn't know about this tradition. I've created a few of my own: "Dinner will be ready when the smoke alarm goes off." "There will always be two choices for dinner, take it or leave it." "Dinner is in the fridge, I'm out."

Or my favorite – "Dinner is in the freezer and the instructions are on the box!" Ladies feel free to use any or all of my dinner suggestions.

One Friday night in particular, I remember that my Mom was going to get Lenny's pizza for dinner. I can picture her as vividly as if it was yesterday. She was standing across the street from our house and I was on the porch. She asked me if I wanted to go with her and I couldn't make up my mind so she started to go without me. Even though dinner was just pizza, there was still a precise time that it had to be on the table. The stopwatch on The Iron Chef or the .0001 second time difference in winning the gold at the Olympics was nothing compared to the sacred time in an Italian family when dinner had to be on the table, so she HAD to go.

After she crossed the street, I called her. She turned. I feel now what I felt then. There was an abyss between us. The one-way street which was probably only 10 steps wide might as well have been the Nile to cross to a preschooler, so I motioned to her. I know in my heart that the silent motion I made to her with my hand in the air her meant, "Mom, please wait a minute for me. I'm going up stairs to get my jacket and something else. I'll be right down. Please wait because, I really, really, really decided and I want to go to Lenny's with you to pick up the pizza for dinner. I'll walk fast because I don't want to slow you down and have dinner on the table late. I promise." So after that silent motion, I ran in the house. I returned in a minute to find my mother gone! She had misinterpreted my silent hand in the air signal as "just go". I was devastated, I cried and was inconsolable. I cried as if I would never see my Mom again even though she was back in no time. Mom, I just needed you to know.

After finishing this particular story, another time that I regret my actions came to mind and it involves both of my parents. Since it took place somewhere between the time I was 5 and Anne's baptism story you are about to read, this is as good a place as any to tell you. My Mom had a hiding place for anything she didn't want us to see. I knew exactly where it was and never told her. When a holiday was coming up or just if I was particularly bored or curious, I would check out the area. Between the armoire that Dad built to match his bedroom furniture and the corner wall in their bedroom, would be "the spot." Sometimes if she was really being secretive for Christmas or birthdays she would use the back of the

inside of the armoire behind Dad's one pair of dress up shoes and covered up by his two dress suits. If I ever found anything in the furniture, I would immediately erase the vision from my mind because I would want to truly act surprised at the time I was supposed to actually receive it.

On one occasion, I found a few rolls of particularly ugly wallpaper – No, I mean really ugly, at least to me. Now, because I wasn't supposed to reveal that I knew the secret hiding place, who was I supposed to confide in and ask what the paper was for? My brother and sister would definitely have told my parents and the fun of knowing about the secret corner stuff would be over, a closed chapter in the fun part of my childhood. So, I just kept quiet and curious.

Guess what? The wallpaper was for my bedroom! Dad must have been on vacation at the time, because one day as soon as I left for school, both of my parents got busy with the surprise they had been planning for me. Hanging wallpaper is no easy task today, so can you imagine what it was like 40 some years ago to paper an entire room in just a few hours? There was no pre-pasted or pre-measured paper. There were rolls of thick immovable paper that required heavy-duty wallpaper paste that needed to be made from scratch. I could only imagine, the second I left for school Dad would jump out of bed, wash up, quickly have his breakfast of a cup of coffee and a Danish, and get started with Mom on the surprise project for me. The furniture would be removed from the room or if too heavy, moved to the side that they were not working on. Perhaps the old wallpaper needed to be soaked and scraped off and the bare walls washed to remove any hard to get off paper and excess glue. Then it needed to be dried and the real work began. The collapsible tin table with the blue-black paisley pattern that we used for company would come out and serve as the worktable. The paste would be made from scratch. Mom and Dad worked as a loving, yelling, smooching team to carefully measure, cut, match patterns, glue, mount and press out the lumps in each piece, but not until everything was perfect would they would proceed to the next section. No doubt, while this work was furiously proceeding, Mom was whipping up some delicacy for dinner while Dad was doing something that he could do alone.

I'm sure each of them was working at top speed and efficiency to ensure that everything would be done before I came home from school so that they could greet me with the big surprise. If I remember correctly,

they were almost done when I came home and went ballistic. "I hope you are kidding me and are going to remove this ugly paper from my walls immediately!" I remember yelling as I threw a fit and had a tantrum in my room. I'm not exactly sure what followed but I'm sure ungrateful, hurt looks and a few sharp remarks were exchanged. I know now what it feels like to spend the entire day doing something for my children and have them come home only to criticize and ridicule me. So, Mom and Dad, "I'm sorry, forgive me."

There was another time when I believe that I hurt my Mom and I wanted to publicly apologize. It may also seem small; however, I have held it in my soul for over 20 years and need to release it. Being pure love and a little bit of a modingine (busybody), Mom always wanted to know exactly what was going on and have a front row view. At my daughter Anne's baptism, the priest was about to pour the Holy Water over her head while she was held over the Baptismal Font. All of a sudden, relatives from my husband's side made a dash for the altar to be close and so did my Mom. Now I couldn't tell my in-laws to sit back down so I told my Mom. It was probably out of sheer frustration. I can see her now. I know she wanted to be right where the action was and I told her to sit. Like a loving obedient puppy with her head down and virtual tail between her legs, she returned to her pew. I know I hurt her. I'm so sorry. I hope you now have a front row view of all the events in your grandchildren's lives.

The Sacred Checkbook

I could never tell which one of my parents was more of a stickler for perfection. I've come to realize that they were equal for those things that mattered to them. No one could layer lasagna as if she was creating the next Picasso or fill and tie a braciole with exquisite love quite like Mom. No one could spend hours and hours and hours hand sanding an unidentified piece of wood that most people would have put in the garbage quite like Dad.

Mom's perfectionism extended outside of cooking. The next thing that Mom held sacred was her checkbook. I know that because after she passed, Dad never changed anything. He didn't remove her name from the account or the checks and more importantly he didn't remove the carefully cut out Anne Lander advice columns, poems of encouragement or prayer cards in the checkbook.

I remember that every week there was the ritual of going to the bank to deposit money and every month there was the ritual of bill paying. The fun part of balancing the account always followed. It was oh so easy back then. She put in X amount and made out checks for Y amount and everything was copasetic, as they would often say. Then came interest on checking accounts and not that it is a bad thing, just confusing to their generation.

It wasn't bad a first, the account balanced. Then one month it didn't and Mom spent hours trying to reconcile what I'm sure was a few cents. It turned out Mom was right and found a mistake that seemed impossible to occur. It was the beginning of digital verification by computer. Each check was verified for accuracy against the deposits and withdrawals to create the monthly statements. It was also the beginning of interest on checking accounts – enough to be interesting, not enough to be valuable, somewhere between "HUH?" and a bit annoying.

Mom's checkbook always, and I mean always, balanced to the penny. If she were alive today running the country, I guarantee we would not have the economic crisis that we are in now. There would be no extra missiles unless they were proven necessary and affordable, no borrowing to get

something we couldn't pay for with cash. No one would get extra money for clothes, cars, or conveniences if what they had was still functioning. We would have no enemies because she would just cook for everyone around the negotiating table and no one would be able to get up until everything was eaten. Then they would all be too full to fight, take a nap and when they got up they would share the leftovers and everyone would go home happy. Alan Greenspan who publicly said that he didn't see the crisis coming had nothing on my Mom. She always balanced our budget and kept everyone full and happy.

However, one time she couldn't balance her checkbook. I remember her spending hours trying, to the point where most people would have given up because it appeared ludicrous, but not to Mom. She checked and double-checked deposits and withdrawals, added in interest, over and over, yet she could not balance her checkbook.

If you look up persistence or tenacity, you'll find a picture of my Mom. I'm sure all of us have had at least one occasion in our lives where we knew we were right and even if the whole world felt otherwise, we were standing our ground. This was Mom's shining moment. I don't exactly remember her eureka moment, but Mom was right! Somewhere between the amounts she wrote on one check and what was digitally created at the bottom of the same check was an error! I'm sure she went right to the bank president to blast him and straighten this out after that her checking account finally balanced.

Before she passed, she was having trouble for a second time balancing her checkbook and asked me several times to help her find the error. I was at the point in my life between juggling being laid off after 20+ years without any compensation or pension and my Mom's illnesses. To me balancing a checkbook was not a priority. I didn't realize how important it was to her. This may sound silly, but after Mom passed, I sat down, went back months in the account and it took hours. I finally found the error and balanced her checkbook.

"Nanny Made" Memories

When my parents got older they started to have multiple medical problems. Reluctantly at first, and then by my lovingly persuasion, they agreed to come and live closer to my sister and I in New Jersey. This meant that we could take care of them better, which gave us peace of mind at a time when both of them needed us more.

Although this time with my parents was a true blessing from God, to be able to be there for them at a time when they needed me, it was a pittance in comparison to all that they did for me and all the times that they were there for me. It was marked by numerous visits to doctors for every organ in their bodies and multiple trips to the emergency room at unexpected times. However, these times of painful necessity were offset by many happy occasions.

My favorite was the impromptu dates that my son, Joseph, who was four at the time, would have with Mom. He adored her. He adored both of my parents and the compliment was returned 100 fold by the "pure love" grandparents. He would call her and ask her if she wanted to go to the movies. She always said, "Yes." My Dad always stayed in their apartment.

If it was summer she would come down in shorts and sunglasses and ask, "Don't I have pretty good gams for an old lady?" Gams, that's what they called glamorous legs during WWII and she did. I can't recall an ounce of cellulite. I wish that I had asked her secret. If it was colder she had her paisley faux down coat on. I never really found out if it was her favorite because she really liked it or if it was her favorite because she fought my Aunt Lee for at a garage sale in Brooklyn. After Mom passed, I wore it for a while because it felt like a hug from her. I gave it to Aunt Lee who has also passed. I hope they are enjoying stories, cigarettes, food, and garage sales in their virtual Brooklyn together in Heaven with Aunt Rosie.

My kids will have many good memories of my parents. However, they may not remember the very sweetest one, the one that for a kid would have locked in just how much they were loved. No matter where we went

together or what we were doing, Mom would always ask to stop at a grocery store before we went home. This was the time that a grandparent would do for their grandchildren what they would never have done for their own children. Mom thought it was a secret from me but I know in her heart she knew that I knew. She would say that she needed my kids to show her where something was in the store so that they would accompany her. One on the right and one on the left, they would go in together. There was no need for me to just run in and get what she needed; she would find it with the kids. What a Grandma – straight to the candy isle. Then my children who were carefully clutched in my Mother's hands were released. "Go get whatever you want and don't tell your Mom." This is the stuff everlasting memories are made of.

Treasures Right Under Your Nose

There was a brown bag that Mom gave me when she moved in with us before her condo was ready. I never opened it. She told me that it was notebooks from when I was in school. After Mom passed, I found it at the bottom of a closet. On one of those very rare occasions when I cleaned, I opened the bag. I wish that I would have opened it while she was still with me because she would have shared great insight into more detail. Perhaps I was meant to open it exactly when I did, a gift from her, a legacy of my Mom's past. Of my brother, sister, and myself my mom knew that if she gave me anything to save, I would be the most likely to keep it. She was right, but little did she know that I would also be the least likely to open it right away.

When I opened that bag, neatly tied together were a few composition books. I'm sure you know that ones that mean. Black and white covers with long sheets of paper folded in half and sewn together with a string to bind the paper to the cover. They have been used for centuries in schools. I expected to find the first book I used in first grade and my first ever homework assignment: to cut out pictures of my family and pets and paste them on the front page. Ah, the 60's, when the family would be a mom, a dad, a sister, a brother, and a dog. I remember doing it. Painstakingly going through Mom's McCall's® and Better Homes & Gardens® magazines and getting permission to cut the pictures I wanted as long as they didn't have a recipe on the back that Mom wanted to cut out and never use. I selected the approved pictures and carefully using the Elmer's school paste that didn't spread, lumped up and left a big hump in your brand new composition book for the entire year, and completed my first ever homework assignment of the 1+ million that followed. What a treasure. Mom had saved my notebook.

Nestled with mine were my brother's and sister's books. Then I found the real treasure, my Mom's composition book from junior high! The book from her Home Economics class was covered with great care in brown paper and contained step-by-step instructions on how to be the best wife. One lesson stands out in my mind: to have the house

cleaned and dinner prepared before your husband came home and to make sure that you were washed and beautified before he stepped though the door after a hard day's work so that you could greet him with a kiss, a newspaper, a drink, and accompany him to his favorite easy chair after a long day at work and give him a massage. Oh the dream of the perfect marriage and illusion of a perfect life, that was shattered by reality of WWII when Mom rivaled Rosie the Riveter. Thank you Mom for being the perfect wife and Mom and the true pioneer that shattered the lead roof that stifled women's rights for centuries.

Order of Dish Washing

1. Glasses
2. Silver
3. Tea pots and saucers
4. Plates
5. Cookery Cutlery
6. Cooking utensils
7. Crockery

Anne and Joseph Continue

There is a tradition that when your children are born out of respect for your parents, you name your kids after them. I am respectful, however, for many reasons I love the names Anne and Joseph. I was fortunate to be the third child born of my parents and that my brother and sister had been named after my grandparents. Actually, by all logical means I should not be here. My Mom had two miscarriages, one before I was born and one after I was born. Perhaps that is why I always felt extra special and extra loved. I could be named whatever my parents wanted me to be named. I was named after them; Joanne – after Joseph and Anne; what a wonderful name. In addition to being blessed to be named after my parents, Joseph is the Virgin Mary's husband and the stepfather of Jesus and Anne is the Mother of the Virgin Mary or Jesus' Grandmother. What a lineage – what a blessing! I'm not telling you this to say by any means that I am a saint, far from it, as all my friends will attest to. However, bearing the name of such noble people holds a big responsibility and I have tried my best to live my life loving and giving as a tribute to my namesakes.

My children were named after my parents. Maybe, just maybe, I named them Anne and Joseph so that I too would be remembered. They have many of my parents' traits. Anne is loving and giving, but God forbid you do something against her and she will never talk to you. I used to say that when her hormones changed going into menopause, my Mom went from Donna Reed to Freddy Krueger, Anne followed in her footsteps as she entered puberty. I stayed at a safe distance until she came out her loving self on the other side.

If you looked up the word stubborn you would probably find a picture of my Dad. He always knew what you wanted. Dad met his match in Joseph. It was a blessing to be able to watch them fight as they worked on projects together. I'm not sure if Dad just gave in or he was no match for his namesake rival because Joseph usually won. You can read this in the story "The Argument and the Neon Green Guitar." Joseph, like my Dad knows exactly what he wants and no one can tell him otherwise. I

just learned to love all the Annes and Josephs that I have been blessed with in my life and it was a great relief to me when I learned to love them "just the way they are." I wouldn't have it any other way.

Anne, Mom, Joseph and Dad
BFF (Best Friends Forever)

Damn the Cholesterol Full Taste Ahead

If Dad's treasures of wood were the feng shui of the rooms he touched in my home, then it was the scent of Mom's cooking, usually heavily scented with garlic, which was the wrapping paper and bow on the present. Mom filled my life with loving food, permeating, melting, and reversing even the worst day or bad attitude with and instant sniff. Her home cooking made warm memories.

If I close my eyes, I can picture Mom in the kitchen, her favorite room. She would be chopping, mixing, have all four burners going and invariably burn herself on the hot oven. She would be wearing a cobbler apron, often hand made by a friend Ellie Pascale or Roz Vartian. It would have a sewed on towel and used tissues in the pockets. Breakfast, lunch, and dinner all going at the same time, the AM transistor radio would be blasting out static and everything was done by the time her favorite TV shows were on or Aunt Rosie called for the daily 8 hour phone call marathon which was free because of party lines. You may not know what a party line is, it's when you share a phone line with some else and if you both pick up at the same time you can just talk. Yes, this meant that someone could listen in on your conversation.

Here are some of Mom's classic recipes that I was fortunate enough to get down on paper because Mom rarely used a recipe or measured anything. This is the first time that I am actually going through Mom's recipe book in detail. Some are in her beautiful script handwriting others are in my printing or typed by me on our manual typewriter. Mom would ask me why I was writing things down as she cooked. "Just watch me," she would say. I wish I had watched more.

The recipes are in no particular order and are not sorted by type. It is the way Mom left them in her recipe book and I wouldn't straighten them out for all the money in the world. I am only including recipes that I believe are my Mom's and unless noted are not from labels or boxes. In case you don't notice immediately, I want to point out that Mom was very aware of the 80/20 rule. However she didn't apply it to do 20% of effort to get 80% of your results. She used it for her own personal food pyramid.

Make sure you have over 80% of the food you eat coming from desserts and throw in daily less than 20% of some meat and cooked veggies with an occasional canned fruit cocktail which you hid the tin taste with a little amaretto or vodka. No wonder I loved fruit cocktail as a kid. It's such a shame the food pyramid was invented and spoiled all the good taste. ENJOY and feel free to improvise!

Joseph and Anne learning the spadini tradition with Nanny.

Recipe Index

I pray that I am doing justice to the translation from Momese.

Amazing Coconut Pie

2 cups milk
¾ cup sugar
½ cup Bisquick®
¼ cup butter
4 eggs
1½ tsp vanilla
1 cup coconut flakes

Combine everything in a blender except coconut. Cover and blend at low speed for 3 min and pour into greased 9" pan. Let stand 5 min. Sprinkle with coconut. Bake 350° for 30-40 min until golden brown. Serve warm or cold.

Beef Soup with Cold Beef and Potato Salad

Carrots – Celery – Onion – Bay Leaf
Can Whole Tomatoes – Salt and Pepper
Potatoes – Stew Meat – Chicken Broth to cover

Clean, peel, chop and cook everything until done.
Remove potatoes and slice when almost cooled.
Flake the meat when cooled. Mix white vinegar and oil as a dressing and toss with meat and potatoes.

Buck Eyes

1 stick butter

2 cups chunky peanut butter

3 cups Rice Krispies®

1 box confectioners' sugar

Mix all ingredients and roll into walnut sized balls.
In double boiler: Melt 12oz chocolate chips and ½ stick butter.
Dip balls in chocolate, 3-4 at a time. Remove with a fork, but don't pierce.
Put on wax paper until set.

Caponatini – Delicious eggplant appetizer

Cut a large onion and brown in oil. Add one can tomato paste and 2 cans of water. Add 3 stalks of celery cut up small. Add a small jar of green olives cut up. Add ½ jar of capers that you have rinsed in cold water to remove the salt. Mix and add ¾ cups wine vinegar and 1 tsp sugar as dressing. Cut a large eggplant into small cubes. Add to the sauce. Mix well and cook ¾ hour. Cook the sauce before time. This is delicious cold or warm with salami and provolone cheese.

Carrot Cake (1)

2 cups flour	1½ cups cooking oil
2 cups sugar	4 eggs
1 tsp salt	3 cups shredded carrots
2 tsp baking soda	½ cup seedless raisins
2 tsp cinnamon	1 cup chopped nuts

Preheat oven at 350°. Sift together dry ingredients. Add oil and eggs. Stir in carrots, raisins, and nuts. Pour into 6 well-greased cans or 2 loaf pans. Fill ⅔ full. Bake for 45-50 min.

Carrot Cake (2)

2 cups unsifted flour, 2 tsp baking soda, 2 tsp cinnamon, ½ tsp ginger, ½ tsp salt, 3 eggs, 1½ cups sugar, ¾ cup mayonnaise, 1 can crushed pineapple with juice, 2 cups grated carrots, 1 cup walnuts, ½ cup raisins.

Grease and flour a pan. Sift first 5 ingredients and set aside. At medium speed, beat next 4 ingredients, and then gradually beat in flour mixture. Stir in carrots, raisins, and walnuts. Pour in pan. Bake 350° for 30-40 min or until tester comes out clean.

Cheese Cake

| 1 lb cream cheese | 1 pt sour cream | 1 cup sugar |
| 5 eggs | 1 tsp vanilla | 1 tsp lemon juice |

Topping ½ cup grated Zwieback®

Mix together: 2 tbsp sugar, 2 tbsp melted butter

Grease a spring pan. Put crumbs on bottom and sides of pan. Separate eggs. Beat cream cheese; add sugar, egg yolks, sour cream, lemon juice, and vanilla. Beat egg whites until stiff. Fold with other ingredients. Place a larger pan of water in the oven. Invert an empty pan in the pan of water, and place the cheese cake pan over the inverted pan to bake over water. Bake 300° for 1 hour. Let stand in oven for ½ hour with the door closed. Let stand in oven for ½ hour with the door open.

Chicken Lemonade

1 can frozen lemonade defrosted in a dish. Add salt, pepper, garlic powder, and parsley. Put in one cut up chicken and let soak for 1 hour. Dip in corn flake crumbs. Drip butter and bake at 350° for 1 hour.

Crescent Cookies (Danish)

1 lb melted butter
4 or more cups non-sifted flour
4 eggs beaten
Any flavor jelly or jam
2 tbsp sugar
3 pkg yeast
½ cup lukewarm water
Mixture of sugar and cinnamon

Dissolve yeast in water. Mix all other ingredients then mix in dissolved yeast. Cover and refrigerate mixture for one hour. Remove the dough and make eight balls. Remove one ball of dough at a time as needed. Roll each ball with a rolling pin over the sugar and cinnamon (not flour). Roll each dough ball round and flat. Cut into 8 slices, like a pie. Place filling on large end of triangle. Roll narrow end to top. Bake 350° for 20-25 min.

Date Nut Bread

<u>Add</u>: 1 tsp. baking soda to ¾ cup of boiling water and 3 tbsp butter.
<u>Add</u>: 1 cup of pitted dates cut in small pieces and 1 cup of walnuts.
<u>Beat</u>: 1 egg and ¾ cup of sugar.
<u>Add</u>: Egg mixture to the first mixture plus 1 tsp of vanilla, 1½ cups of flour and ½ tsp salt.
Mix well and turn into a loaf pan or for round loaf use a coffee can for baking.
Bake in 350° oven for 45 min.

Dump Cake – From Fran

Lightly grease a 9"x13" pan
Do not mix
Dump into pan
1 can crushed pineapple
1" cherry pie filling
Spread 1 package of cake mix
Melt one cup of margarine
Pour over
Sprinkle 1½ cups chopped nuts
Bake 350° for 1 hour
Top with whipped cream

One Bowl Orange Coffee Cake

6 oz can frozen orange juice concentrate thawed
2 cups flour
½ cup soft butter
1 cup sugar
½ cup milk
⅓ cup chopped walnuts
Topping: ⅓ cup sugar, ¼ cup walnuts, 1 tsp cinnamon.
Bake: 350° for 45 min.

1 tsp baking flour
2 eggs
1 tsp salt
1 cup raisins

In a large mixing bowl, combine ½ cup of the juice with flour, sugar, soda, salt, butter, milk, eggs, raisins, and nuts. Blend on low speed of electric mixer for 30 sec. Beat for 3 min at medium speed until well blended. Pour into a well greased and floured 9"x13" baking pan. Bake. Remove pan to wire rack. Drizzle with remaining orange juice while still warm. Sprinkle with topping. Cut into squares or bars to serve.

Pepper Steak

1¼ lbs tender beef (Top sirloin, London broil or Flank steak)

2 lbs fresh green peppers

¼ tsp accent

3 tbsp cornstarch

3 tbsp oil

1 clove crushed garlic

1½ to 2 cups bouillon

salt & pepper to taste

½ tsp powdered ginger

2 tbsp soy sauce

2 cups cooked rice

Cut beef into ⅛" slices – cut each pepper into 8 pieces. Mix starch, accent and soy sauce in ¼ cup cold water, set aside. Place oil, salt, pepper, ginger and garlic in hot skillet. Add beef, sauté 10 min, add green peppers and mix well. Add all ingredients except starch mixture. Mix thoroughly, lower gas and cook 10 min. Add starch mixture, stir until it thickens – serve over rice. Serves 4.

Poppy Seed Bread

3 cups flour

1½ tsp baking powder

1½ cups milk

1½ tbsp poppy seeds

1½ tsp vanilla

1½ tsp salt

2½ cups sugar

1⅛ cup salad oil

3 eggs

1½ tsp almond extract

Glaze – ¾ cups sugar, ¼ cup orange juice, 2 tsp melted butter, ½ tsp vanilla, ½ tsp almond extract

Mix together while bread is baking

Mix everything together. Beat two minutes with electric beater. Pour into greased and floured loaf pans for about 1¼ hours. Remove from pans immediately. Place on cookie sheet. Spoon and re–spoon glaze over warm bread until it hardens. Enjoy.

Sour Cream Cake – From Roz with Mom's improvising

<u>Cream Together:</u> ¼ lb butter and ¾ cup sugar .
<u>Add:</u> 2 eggs and 1 tsp vanilla
<u>Sift together, set aside for last:</u> 2 cups flour, 1 tsp baking powder, 1 tsp baking soda, and ½ tsp salt
<u>Add:</u> 1 cup sour cream
Butter ring pan. Pour ½ batter and add some topping, add remaining batter, then remaining topping.
<u>Topping:</u> ½ cup sugar, 1 cup chopped walnuts, 1 tsp. cinnamon, and ¼ cup chocolate chips
Bake 350° for 45 min. Batter will be thick.

Spicy Carrot Cake

1½ cups salad oil	4 egg yolks
4 egg whites	2½ cups sifted flour
1½ tsp baking powder	¼ tsp salt
1 tsp cinnamon	5 tbsp hot water
1¾ cups grated raw carrots	1 tbsp lemon juice
2½ cups granulated sugar	½ tsp baking soda
1 tsp nutmeg	1 tsp ground cloves
1 cup chopped pecans	¾ cup sifted confectioners' sugar

Early in the day:

1. Start heating oven to 350°. Grease well then flour a 10" heavy cast aluminum Bundt® cake pan.
2. In a large bowl, with electric mixer at medium speed, cream the oil and sugar until well mixed. Then beat in egg yolks, one at a time, beating well after each addition. Now beat in hot water.
3. Sift together flour, baking powder, baking soda, salt, nutmeg, cinnamon, and cloves; beat into egg mixture
4. Now, into batter stir 1½ cups grated carrots, then pecans. Next beat egg whites until soft peaks form; then fold into batter.
5. Turn into prepared pan and bake for 60–70 min or until a cake tester, inserted into the center, comes out clean. Cool in pan for 15 min, then remove from the pan and finish cooling on a wire rack.
6. Make a glaze this way: Combine sifted confectioners' sugar with lemon juice. Use to drizzle in circle on top of cake. Then sprinkle glaze with remaining ¼ cup grated raw carrots.
7. Serve on a pretty plate, cut into wedges. Cake keeps well when wrapped and refrigerated. Or if preferred, cover with freezer wrap and freeze.

Stuffed Cabbage

Par boil cabbage separate leaves
1 lb chop meat
4 stalks celery
1 cup cooked rice
1 large can tomatoes
2 onions
Saturate in mayonnaise
Seasonings
Make a plain tomato sauce

Mix all ingredients. Roll in the leaves. Place in a pan and cover with the sauce.
Bake 350° for over ½ hour.

Sugar Doughnuts

Crisco® for shallow frying
¼ cup sugar
2 cups buttermilk pancake mix
1 cup milk
1 egg
Cinnamon and sugar or confectioners' sugar

Melt enough Crisco® (or oil) for 1" deep layer in a deep pan. Heat to 365°. Combine pancake mix and sugar. Add milk and egg. Stir just until pancake mix is moistened. At once, drop a few spoonfuls at a time in the hot Crisco®. Brown on both sides, then drain on a paper towel. Roll in the cinnamon and sugar or confectioners' sugar.

Sunshine Cheese Cake

2 cups graham cracker crumbs
⅓ cup sugar
¾ cup sugar
2 tbsp flour
1 tsp vanilla
½ cup melted butter
3 (8 oz.) packages softened cream cheese
2 tbsp cornstarch
6 egg yolks
6 egg whites, beaten
1 cup orange juice

Mix graham crackers, butter and ⅓ cup sugar. Press in pan for crust.
Blend other ingredients for cake and pour in pan.
Bake 350° for 45 min. Let cool for 1 hour.

Swedish Rice Pudding

4 cups milk
½ cup sugar
3 tbsp sugar
4 egg yolks
4 egg whites

½ tsp salt
1 tsp vanilla
½ cup long grain rice
2 tsp butter, softened

In a large sauce pan bring milk to boiling, but not foaming.
Stir in rice and salt. Heat medium low. Cook uncovered 18 min. Combine
yolks, ½ cup sugar, butter, and vanilla. Beat, but not foamy. Stir 1 cup
rice into the egg mixture. Then put back into pot. Boil 1 min. Beat egg
whites and sugar. Top with egg whites and bake 350° for 15 min.

Twist Cookies – Thanks Roz

<u>Beat in a bowl</u>: 4 eggs, ¼ cup water, 2 tsp vanilla, add 1 cup sugar
<u>Melt</u>: 1 cup Crisco® and 1 cup oleo margarine
8 cups flour
2 tsp baking powder
½ tsp. salt

Mix by hand until doughy. Keep warm ½ hour. Take small amounts of dough, roll and form twist. Set on a cookie sheet. Brush with egg. Sprinkle with sesame seeds. 350° oven. Bake until golden brown.

Walnut Pinwheels

Yield: 8
Preheat oven 350°
9" pie plate
1 pkg crescent rolls

Filling: ½ cup sugar
      ½ cup chopped walnuts
      ⅓ cup brown sugar
      1 tsp cinnamon
      2 tsp melted butter

Topping: ⅓ cup confectioners' sugar
      1 tbsp cold milk
      ½ tsp almond extract

Mix sugar, brown sugar, cinnamon, and walnuts in a bowl. Brush one side of individual crescents with butter. Place generous amount of filling on crescent and roll in crescent fashion. Place crescents in pinwheel style in pie plate. Sprinkle remainder of filling mixture over crescents. Bake 25-30 min until center is done. Cool crescents; dribble topping over surface in circular motion – Serve.

Just this morning, on November 2, 2008, I came across another tin box full of Mom's recipes. I had spray painted an old index card tin for her in 1985 and I was supposed to decorate it as a special Christmas present, in a vain attempt at my being Artsie Fartsie or as it has become known as Foo Foo. I spray-painted it alright and as of some 22 plus years later it has not been decorated. I guess that I was busy. Mom in her infinite love used it any way and overstuffed it with delish. So, here are some additional buried treasure recipes from the red box. The box has alphabetical index cards that Mom hand wrote and many letters are missing and they are all out of order. The recipes are all yellow, not carefully folded, mostly hand written. Some are written on the back of other papers. Mom was a pioneer in recycling. I found an invitation to come to the New Bingo Game at the Congregation B'Nai Jacob on Glenwood Road and East 31st, right on our corner. Opening Day was Tuesday Nov. 7 Election Day – with free coffee on opening day. How ironic. Tomorrow is Election Day 2008. The invitation must be 50 years old! Recipes are on the back of Rheingold® Beer Ads and many Dear Abby columns that she read from the Brooklyn Daily News. Wow, what a treasure! For those of you who like clues and would like to date some of these recipes, on the back of one is an ad from a grocery store circular that has rib steaks for $1.79 a pound.

I found a section of the TV guide from the Daily News. Even though the section had no heading I know it was the Daily News because we were only allowed that paper in the house. I firmly believed all other papers were Communist papers. There was the daily TV line up. By day, there is only a max of 7 stations beginning at 5:50AM with the news. No 24-hour TV. There is a max of 7 stations during the day: 2, 4, 5, 7, 9, 11 and an occasional 68. At night was the big selection: 8, with Washington Week in Review simultaneously on channels 50, 52, and 58 and an occasional movie station. Kids today don't know what they are missing, with all this variety on TV, how could we be bored? Sometimes we were bored, really bored and we would get up, yes get up, no remotes in those days, and manually change the channel on the channel knob and find a station that was not broadcasting anything but static and watch the snow! How ironic, in the middle of all these delicious fattening and >80% dessert recipes, I found a Cholesterol Control and Salt-free Diet Plan for my Dad from December 7, 1981. December 7, the day Pearl Harbor was attacked and the day my Dad tried to attack his cholesterol, both to no avail.

Mom must have used this tin for other purposes because there are a bunch of prayer cards from funerals and one of the tabs was marked O.W. and Alms. I think this is where Mom kept track of what she might have borrowed and needed to return to others. She often put things in unexpected places to fool potential thieves. I once found a stack of money wrapped in foil in the back of the freezer and Mom's money clearly marked in her underwear drawer! I believe that thieves have moms too and that is the first place they would look for the family jewels when they come to rob you. Thank God we were never robbed and Mom's O.W. (IOU) & Alms section was empty. I'm blessed that I found this tin today while writing the recipe section so that I can preserve Mom's gold and share them with you. I carefully took them out in the order that they are in the tin. DOUBLE ENJOY!

How wonderful. Mom helped me write the ending for this section. I know it is the ending because I marked the spot with an adorable hand sewed felt and lace mitten surrounding a hair clip.

The last piece of folded up yellow paper was a letter to the editor that follows.
It's perfect...here are some excerpts.
Thank you Mom.

A Trip Down Memory Lane

Nostalgia: What was, is no more.
Butter had a superior taste,
    when carved and sold from wooden tubs
Fountain pens refilled in banks and post offices,
    with ink blotters
Cacophony of cow bells announcing the junkman
Ice cream mello–rolls...Girls played Jacks...
    Boys played skelly
Mom and pop grocery stores...Assembly day in school
The daredevil was the clothesline installer
...Large metal pans were under the ice box
Families cared for aging relatives
Your relatives were in walking distance and
Sunday was visiting day

Red Tin Recipe Treasures

Sesame Cookies 87
Carrot Cake 87
Almond Cookies 88
Anise Flavored Cookies. 88
Apple Oatmeal Pie. 89
Apple Fritters 90
Angel Food Cake 91
Beer Batter 91
Bread Sticks 92
Butter Balls. 92
Powdered Sugar Bows. 92
Ricotta Turnovers 93
Brown Sugar Squares 93
Cheese Ball 94
Eight Minute Cheese Cake. . . . 94
Crinkle Pastry with Syrup 94
Chicken Capolatina. 95
Apple Butter Cake. 95
Tomato Cake 96
Butter Cookies Rolled. 96
Chocolate Cici Cookies. 97
Chocolate Syrup Cake. 98
Viennese Crescents 98
Cream Puffs 99
Mom's Cheese Cake. 99
Cheese Cake 100
Wine Cake 101
Fig Cookies 101
Zucchini Hot Cakes 102
Date Nut Kisses. 102
Mace Cake. 103
Creamy Orange Frosting. 103
Kahlua 104

Potato Filling Casserole. 104
Peanut Butter Cookies 105
Oatmeal Date Squares 105
Sweet and Sour Pineapple
Pork 106
Pina Colada Cake. 107
Rice Fritters 107
Sesame Seed Rings 108
Bread and Cheese Soup. 108
Struffoli. 109
Ministrone Soup 110
Anne's Pound Cake 110
Zucchini Pie 111

86

Sesame Cookies

350° oven
3 cups flour
1 tsp baking powder
1 cup sugar
3 eggs beaten
Sesame seeds

1 tsp salt
Sift together
2 sticks butter
1 tsp vanilla

Mix and knead. Dip in milk. Roll in seeds. Bake.

Carrot Cake

2 cups unsifted flour – 2 tsp baking soda
2 tsp cinnamon – ½ tsp ginger – ½ tsp salt
3 eggs – 1½ cups sugar – ¾ cup mayo
1 can 8 oz crushed pineapple, with juice
2 cups grated carrots – 1 cup walnuts – ½ cup raisins

Grease and flour the pan.
Sift first 5 ingredients. Set aside.
At medium speed, beat next 5 ingredients. Gradually beat in flour mixture. Stir in carrots, raisins, and walnuts. Pour in the pan and bake 350° for 30-40 min or until tester comes out clean.

Almond Cookies (twice baked)

½ cup corn oil

3 eggs

1½ tsp baking powder

1 tbsp almond extract

½ cup sugar

2 cups flour

½ cup almonds

1 tbsp vanilla extract

Mix all together by hand. Place dough in refrig over night. Shape like 2 loaves of French bread. Bake at 350° for 15 min. Take out of oven. Cut ½" thick slices and put back on tray, cut side up. Bake 15 min on each side or until golden brown.

Anise Flavored Cookies

6 eggs

1 tsp vanilla

6 tsp baking powder

½ lb margarine (melted)

1 cup sugar

5 cups of flour (or more)

Beat eggs, add sugar. Mix well; add margarine, vanilla, baking powder, and flour. Roll out in small pieces, shape. Bake 350° for 10 min or until golden brown. Make confectioners' sugar icing adding ¼ tsp anise extract. Coat cookies and sprinkle with a little confetti.

Apple Oatmeal Pie

FILLING:
6-8 apples peeled and sliced thin
2 cups sugar
⅓ cup tapioca
Enough water to cover the apples
2 tbsp butter
3 tbsp lemon juice
2 tbsp cinnamon

TOPPING: (enough to make crumbs)
1 cup flour
1 cup instant oatmeal
½ cup brown sugar
3 tbsp butter

Make a pie crust

Cook apple filling until thickened. Put cooked apples in uncooked crust, dot with butter, cover with crumbs topping. Balk 350° 30-35 min. Drizzle confectioners' sugar and a little water over cold pie.

Apple Fritters

Batter: 2 cups sifted flour
                1 pint (2 cups) beer at room temperature
Apples: 5 medium tart cooking apples
                1 cup sugar
                1 tbsp cinnamon
                Oil, confectioners' sugar

Sift the flour into a deep mixing bowl and make a well in the center. Slowly, pour in the beer and stirring gently, gradually incorporate the flour. Continue to stir until the mixture is smooth, but do not beat or over mix. Set the batter to rest at room temp for 3 hours.

15 min before making fritters, peel and core the apples, cut into ⅓" rounds. Lay the rounds side by side on wax paper. Then combine the sugar and cinnamon in a small bowl and sprinkle the mixture evenly over both sides of each apple round.

Preheat the oven on lowest setting. Line a large shallow pan with double thickness of paper toweling and set it in the middle of the oven. Pout oil in frying pan about 3"deep.

Immerse each apple slice, one at a time in the batter and when it is well coated on both sides, drop it into the hot oil. Fry fritters for 4 min turning occasionally until evenly browned. Then transfer to paper lined pan to keep warm. Sprinkle with confectioners' sugar.

Angel Food Cake

1 cup flour
1⅓ cups egg whites (12 at room temperature)
1¼ tsp cream of tartar
½ tsp vanilla

1½ cups sugar

¼ tsp salt
½ tsp almond extract

Mix cream of tartar and salt, beat into egg whites. Beat until they are stiff, not dry. Sprinkle over ¾ cup sugar a teaspoon at a time add the extract flavorings. Mix in flour and ¾ cup sugar. Bake 325° for 1 hour.

Beer Batter

1¼ cups beer
2 tbsp parmesan cheese
1 tsp salt
1 tbsp olive oil
2 stiff-beaten egg whites

1⅓ cups flour, sifted
1 tbsp parsley
dash garlic powder
2 beaten egg yolks
cooking oil

Let the beer stand at room temperature 45 min or until flat. In a mixing bowl, combine flour, parmesan cheese, parsley, salt, and garlic powder. Stir in olive oil, egg yolks, and flat beer; beat until smooth. Fold in stiff-beaten egg whites. Dip vegetables or meat in batter. Fry in deep hot oil, until golden brown. 2-5 min. Drain on paper and serve immediately. Makes 3 cups batter.

Bread Sticks

7 cups flour
1 tsp salt
3 cups or more milk

½ lb butter (melt)
½ yeast cake (melt in warm milk)

Rest 4-5 hours. Shape like Twist. Dip in eggs.
Roll in sesame seeds. Bake 375° for ½ hour.

Butter Balls

Cream 1 cup (2 sticks) butter and ½ cup confectioners' sugar until fluffy. Blend in ½ tsp vanilla and 1¾ cups sifted flour; stir in ½ cup chopped nuts. Chill several hours for ease in handling. Shape into balls 1" in diameter; place on baking sheet at 350° for 20 min. Roll warm in confectioners' sugar. Makes 3 dozen.

Powdered Sugar Bows

3 eggs
¼ cup oil
½ cup sugar

1 tbsp baking powder
2½ cups flour
1 tsp vanilla

Mix all ingredients well in above order. Roll in small pieces. Cut into rectangles and twist into bow shapes. Deep fry. Cool and add powdered sugar.

Ricotta Turnovers

3 lb of ricotta

2 lb of flour

1 tsp very full of Crisco®

⅓ cup of sugar

1½ cups of water

Fix your ricotta the way you like it then refrigerator it until you are ready. Mix flour with melted Crisco® in a pot, work well for 10-15 min, rubbing between hands flour and Crisco®.

Melt sugar in warm water and add to flour with Crisco® work around until it leaves the pot clean, then take it out of the pot, put it on a board and knead well, when done keep it covered with dish then take out a little at a time and roll out thin and start making your turn over when you have 8-10 ready start frying them make sure that they are sealed good and will not open while frying.

Brown Sugar Squares

1 egg, unbeaten

1 tsp vanilla

¼ tsp baking soda

1 cup coarsely chopped walnuts

1 cup brown sugar, packed

½ cup sifted all-purpose flour

¼ tsp salt

Grease 8" square pan. Stir together the egg, brown sugar and vanilla. Quickly stir in flour, soda, and salt. Add walnuts. Spread in pan and bake at 350°, 18-20 min. Don't over bake. Cookies should be soft in the center when taken from the oven. Cool in pan; cut in squares. Makes 16 – 2" squares.

Cheese Ball

8 oz cream cheese soften
4 oz blue cheese soften
Dash Worcestershire Sauce
Chopped walnuts
Roll ball in walnuts and put in wax paper – keep in refrig

Eight Minute Cheese Cake

8 oz cream cheese
1 cup sour cream
8 oz Cool Whip® thawed

⅓ cup sugar
2 tsp vanilla
1 graham cracker crust

Beat cheese until smooth. Beat in sugar. Blend in sour cream and vanilla. Fold in a container of Cool Whip® blending well. Spoon into crust. Chill for 4 hours. Garnish with strawberries.
For chocolate cake, mix 1" square semi-sweet chocolate.

Crinkle Pastry with Syrup (Thanks Roz)

Lay filo dough flat. Dab with melted butter and sprinkle with nuts. Roll on one stick loosely, and press both ends towards center. Holding one end, pull stick out. Pour melted butter over the top before placing in the oven. Cook at 350° for 20 min until golden brown.

Syrup – 1 cup water, 2 cups sugar. Cook until thick. Pour over cooled cookies and before serving.

Chicken Capolatina

Brown chicken pieces – then brown onion – add 1 can capolatina and 1 can mushrooms – salt, pepper, and parsley add 1 can chicken – broth – bring to a boil – put in chicken and cook 1 hour.

Apple Butter Cake

Oven: 350°, 9" square baking pan greased

½ cup melted butter

¾ cup brown sugar

1 tsp cinnamon

1 tsp vanilla

1 egg

1½ cups flour

1 tsp baking soda

½ tsp salt

1 cup apple butter

½ cup chopped raisins

Combine with the butter in a saucepan, mix well
Pour into greased baking pan.

¼ cup sugar

¼ cup flour

¼ tsp nutmeg

½ cup chopped nuts

¼ cup brown sugar

¼ tsp cinnamon

¼ cup softened butter

Combine in a bowl until crumbly and sprinkle over cake.
Bake 40-45 min.

Tomato Cake

2 tbsp butter

1 egg beat well

1 tsp cinnamon

½ tsp nutmeg

1 cup raisins

½ tsp baking soda

1 cup sugar

2 cups flour

½ tsp mace

3 tsp baking powder

1 can tomato soup

Dissolve ½ tsp soda in the soup before adding to mixture.

Icing: 1 box confectionary sugar, 1 tbsp butter, warm milk about ¼ to ½ cup and heat quickly. Add vanilla to taste.

Butter Cookies Rolled

1 lb butter

2 eggs

½ tsp baking powder

2 cups sugar

3½ or more of flour – about 5 cups is right

Vanilla

Mix. Roll very thin. Brush with egg. Bake 350° until golden brown.

Chocolate Cici Cookies (Garbanzo Beans)

Don't use canned cici because they have salt. Soak ¾ lb of cici in hot water over night. In the morning start cooking them with low flame, add water as needed. Cook them well until they are very soft, about ½ hour. Before you close the gas, add ½ tsp of baking soda. After ½ hour, close gas. Drain all water then with a potato masher, mash the cici very well. In a pot, melt 1¼ cup of honey, low gas, when the honey has boiled a few min, add cici, mix well. Then add ¾ lb shredded chocolate (plain milk chocolate). Mix well again, and then add 1¼ tsp of cinnamon. Mix well again. Put all this in a bowl and cover very well. This can stay in refrigerator about 2 or more weeks, so you can make this in advance.

Dough:

2 lbs flour	¾ cup peanut oil or Crisco® for frying
1½ tsp vanilla	6 eggs
1½ cups sugar	½ cup white wine
¾ tsp baking powder	

Mix well. On a board spread with a rolling stick. Put 1 tbsp of the cici mix about 1" apart. Cover with dough and cut around with a roller, like a ravioli. Then, with the tip of the fork, make sure your press all around the cake (but make sure you don't cut the dough with the fork). When this is done, make 3 holes on top of cake (3 times with the fork) to let air out as it cooks.

Then fry in Crisco® (or peanut oil) in a deep fryer make sure the Crisco® is very hot before you put the cakes in. When light, drain on paper towels. When the cakes are lukewarm, sprinkle with powdered sugar.

Chocolate Syrup Cake

¼ lb butter or margarine
1 cup sugar – cream together well
4 eggs one at a time
1 cup flour – sifted
1 tsp baking powder
1 lb can chocolate syrup

Mix together – pour in a greased Bundt pan.
Bake for 45 min (no longer) at 350°.
Could also be baked in a large square pan.

Viennese Crescents

Combine the following:
1 cup ground walnuts
¾ cup sugar
1½ tsp vanilla extract

1 cup butter or margarine
2½ cups sifted flour

Knead dough smooth and shape about 1 tsp of dough at a time into small crescents. Bake on an ungreased cookie sheet in a moderate oven 350° until slightly brown about 15 min. While still warm, roll in vanilla sugar. When completely cool roll again.

Vanilla Sugar:
1 lb box of confectioners' sugar sifted and vanilla powder and mix. Let stand. Then start your crescents.

Cream Puffs

1 cup sifted flour
½ cup Crisco®

1 cup boiling water
3 eggs

Bring water to a boil and add Crisco®. Take away from heat and flour and mix, and then add 1 egg at a time and mix. Place spoonfuls of dough on a baking pan. Put in a very hot oven 400° for 10 min and then reduce heat to 350° and bake for 20 min more. That will be ½ hour all together.

Fill with a combination of vanilla pudding and whipped cream.

Mom's Cheese Cake

4 – 8oz whipped cream cheese
1¼ cup sugar
1 tsp lemon juice
1¼ tsp vanilla

¼ lb sweet butter
16 oz sour cream
2 tbsp corn starch
5 eggs

Let cream cheese, sour cream, butter and eggs stand at room temperature for one hour.

Blend cream cheese, butter and sour cream together, and then add corn starch, sugar, vanilla and lemon juice. Beat on whip speed until well blended. Beat in one egg at a time until the entire mixture is very smooth.

Pour mixture into a greased 9½" spring pan, place pan in a large roasting pan half filled with warm water. Bake 375° for one hour, turn off oven and let cool with oven door open for one hour then take cake out.

Let stand at room temperature for two hours then cover and refrigerate for at least six hours.

Cheese Cake

Preheat oven to 325°

Crust
Use 1½ cups Zwieback® crumbs
¼ cup sugar
4 tbsp butter melted
Mix together and line bottom and sides of pan – chill

Cake Ingredients
3 – 8 oz pkgs cream cheese softened   16 oz sour cream
8 oz heavy cream   1 cup sugar
4 eggs   1 tbsp grated lemon rind
½ tsp vanilla   ½ tsp almond extract

1. Cream the softened cream cheese – slowly cream in 1 cup sugar until smooth.
2. Beat in eggs 1 at a time
3. Stir in sour cream
4. Beat heavy cream until slightly thick (not whipped)
5. Add other ingredients
6. Add lemon peel and extracts
7. Pour into crust
8. Bake 1 hour 25 min 325°

Leave in oven – door closed 1 hour longer
Cool on rack – remove outside of pan
Put on topping – cherry – blueberry – pineapple (whatever)
Cool in refrigerator until ready to use.

Wine Cake

1 pkg yellow cake mix –
1 pkg instant vanilla pudding
¾ cup dry or cream sherry
Confectioners' sugar

1 tsp nutmeg
¼ cup cooking oil
4 eggs

Combine cake mix, pudding, sherry, oil, eggs and nutmeg in a large bowl. Beat 5 min, at medium speed. Grease and flour 10" tube pan. Pour in batter. Bake 350° oven for one hour. Cool on wire rack and sprinkle with confectioners' sugar.

Fig Cookies

<u>Dough:</u>
Mix first: 1 lb sugar
Mix in: 2 ½ lb flour
6 egg yolks (save the whites)
1 tsp vanilla

1½ cup warm milk
1½ lb Crisco®
8 tsp baking powder

<u>Filling:</u> 1½ ropes of figs (soak in warm water) chopped 1 lb almonds, toasted, chopped – ½ lb honey – ½ tsp cinnamon – ¼ lb chocolate chopped – Grate ½ orange rind. Roll dough, fill, bake 350° for 10 min. When warm, cover with topping.
<u>Top:</u> Beat egg whites and powdered sugar.

Zucchini Hot Cakes

1½ grated zucchini (pressed dry with a paper towel)
2 tbsp grated onion
¼ cup grated cheese
¼ cup flour
2 eggs
2 tbsp mayo
¼ tsp oregano
Salt and Pepper
Mix together, fry

Date Nut Kisses

Beat 2 egg whites very stiff, add gradually 1½ cups of confectioners' sugar, and continue beating until firm and glossy.

Fold in 1 cup of pitted dates cut in small pieces, and ½ cup walnuts.

Drop from teaspoon in lightly greased cookie sheet. Bake in 250° oven for 9 min.

Mace Cake

2 cups sifted flour
2 tsp baking powder
⅔ cup shortening
3 eggs
Grated rind from 1 orange

½ tsp salt
¾ tsp ground mace
1⅓ cups sugar
⅔ cup milk

Sift the first 4 ingredients together and set aside for later. Cream shortening and sugar together until fluffy. Beat in eggs, one at a time. Beginning and ending with flour, add flour mixture alternately with milk. About ⅓ of each at a time, add orange rind to the batter. Beat 20 strokes after all ingredients are added.

Pour batter into a well greased, lightly floured 8"x3" tube pan. Bake in a moderate oven 350° for 50 min or until a cake tester comes out clean. Cool 10 min in the pan. Turn out onto wire rack to finish cooling. Frost with Creamy Orange Frosting.

Creamy Orange Frosting

¼ cup softened butter
¼ tsp grated lemon rind
1 egg white

1½ cups confectioners' sugar
1 tsp grated orange rind
2 tbsp fresh orange juice

Beat butter with a spoon until fluffy. Gradually add one cup of the sugar. Add lemon and orange rinds. In a separate bowl, beat egg whites until they stand in soft peaks. Gradually beat in the remaining sugar. Blend into first mixture. Stir in orange juice.

Kahlua

2 cups water
2 cups sugar
24 oz vodka

¼ cup instant coffee
3" vanilla bean
½ gallon bottle

Bring water to a boil then add coffee and sugar, let cool. Pour in the bottle add vanilla bean and vodka. Shake every day for a month.

Potato Filling Casserole

2 cups mashed potatoes
1½ cups milk
3 eggs
¼ cup chopped parsley

3 tbsp butter
4 slices of white bread cubed
½ cup chopped onion
½ tsp salt

Preheat oven to 375°. Grease a 2 quart casserole. In a large bowl, mix potatoes, milk, eggs, parsley, and salt. In a medium skillet, in hot butter, cook bread cubes and onion until they are browned. Stir into potato mixture. Pour into casserole. Bake 1 hour or until top is browned. Serves 6.

Peanut Butter Cookies

14oz can sweetened condensed milk
2 cups Bisquick®
¾ cup peanut butter

1 tsp vanilla extract
Granulated sugar

Preheat oven to 375°. In a large mixer bowl, beat milk and peanut butter until smooth. Add Bisquick® and vanilla, mix well. Shape into 1" balls. Roll in sugar. Place 2" apart on an ungreased baking sheet. Flatten with a fork. Bake 6-8 min or until lightly browned. Don't over bake. Cool and store tightly covered at room temperature.

To add chocolate candy kiss, shape round, but don't flatten. Bake. Press kiss in center immediately after baking.

Oatmeal Date Squares

Filling: ½ lb box pitted dates, cut up; ½ cup brown sugar; ¾ cup water; ½ tsp vanilla. Cook until smooth. Cool while mixing the rest.

1 cup brown sugar; ¾ cup butter; 1¾ cups fine oatmeal; 1½ cups flour; 1 tsp baking powder; ½ tsp salt

Rub dry ingredients and butter together until fine. Save out 1½ cups of mixture. Press the rest in an 8"x12" pan. Cover with filling, and then cover with remaining mixture. Bake 20 min at 365°. Cut in squares while warm.

Sweet and Sour Pineapple Pork

4 medium size pork chops (or beef, chicken or shrimp)
4 oz sweet mixed pickles, drained (save juice)
8oz can pineapple tidbits, drained (save juice)

1 oz bamboo shoots   ½ oz snow peas
1 clove garlic   2 cups oil for deep frying
1 tbsp corn starch   4 tbsp soy sauce
1 tbsp sherry   6 sliced water chestnuts
2 tbsp cold water   ½ tsp salt

Cut pork chops into 1" squares. Marinate 20 min in a mixture of 2 tbsp soy sauce, 1 tbsp sherry, ½ tsp salt. Wash and cut snow peas and par boil. Cut large pickles in half. Fry the meat 7-10 min. Drain and keep warm.

Sauce: Crush garlic. Heat 1 tbsp oil, add garlic. Slowly add the juice from the pineapple and pickles. Add 2 tbsp of soy sauce and bring to a boil. When boiling, add bamboo shoots, water chestnuts, pineapple and pickles. Dissolve cornstarch in cold water and add to sauce mixture to thicken it. Just before serving mix in snow peas. Pour the sauce over the warm pork and serve immediately.

Pina Colada Cake

1 box white cake mix
1 pkg instant coconut cream pudding
4 eggs
1/3 cup rum

1/2 cup water
1/4 cup oil

Mix all ingredients. Grease and flour pan. Bake 350° for 30 min to 1 hour until done. Cool and cut in 2 layers.

Frosting and filling:
8 oz can crushed pineapple
1/3 cup rum
1 pkg instant coconut pudding
9 oz frozen whipped topping
1 bag flaked coconut

Mix pineapple, pudding and rum until smooth. Add whipped topping, stir gently. Sprinkle coconut on top and side.

Rice Fritters

2½ cups cold cooked rice
¾ cup flour
¼ cup sugar
3 eggs
Salad oil

¼ tsp nutmeg
1 pkg active dry yeast
2 tsp grated lemon peel
½ tsp salt
Confectioners' sugar

In a large bowl with mixer at medium speed, beat rice and all ingredients except oil and sugar. Cover bowl and let stand in a warm place 1 hour. In a large pan, heat oil and drop batter by tbsp and fry until golden brown. Drain and sprinkle with sugar. Serve warm.

Sesame Seed Rings

8 oz pkg cream cheese
3 cups flour
½ cup sesame seeds

½ lb butter
½ tsp salt

Let cream cheese and butter be at room temp, stir with wooden spoon until blended. Add flour, salt. Mix by hand until dough is formed. Place in bowl, cover and let stand 1 hour. Roll dough ½" thick on lightly floured board. Cut in 3" circle and cut smaller circle in center and remove center. Pour sesame seeds into plate and gently dip both sides into seeds and place rings on greased cookie sheet. Bake 325° for 35-40 min.

Bread and Cheese Soup

Sauté 3 chopped garlics in a little oil. Add 2 chicken bouillon and 2 cups of water. Boil. Beat in 1 egg. Cut up two slices of bread and add in with parsley. Place in a pan and top with Swiss cheese and brown in oven until cheese melts.

Struffoli

4 egg yolks

4 tbsp sugar

1 tbsp white vinegar

3 tbsp rye, whisky or bourbon

2 cups flour

1 tsp baking powder

Oil for deep frying

almonds

Candied cherries

2 egg whites

4 tbsp corn oil

1 tsp vanilla

¼ tsp salt

1 cup honey

⅔ cup blanched, oven toasted

Rainbow sprinkles

1. Beat together egg yolks, whites and sugar. Beat in oil, vinegar, whisky, and vanilla. Add flour, salt and baking powder and mix into soft dough. Add extra flour if necessary to make it workable. Knead dough for a few min on a lightly floured board. Roll into two balls. Keep one wrapped in refrigerator while you work with the other.

2. Take handfuls of dough and roll into snakes, about the thickness of a chickpea. Cut into uniform chickpea size pieces and set aside on wax paper.

3. Heat several inches of oil in a deep pan. Use a fry basket or slotted spoon to lower dough in and out of hot oil. Oil is hot enough when a piece of dough bobs to the surface and browns in a minute. Cook a few pieces of dough at a time, giving them space to puff and roll evenly to brown. Remove and drain on paper bags.

4. Pour honey into a large pan and bring to a boil over gentle heat. Cook for about 4 min until lightly caramelized and a little deeper in color. Remove from heat. Add struffoli and almonds. Mix well to coat.

5. When cool enough to handle, mound onto a plate or place individual portions in cup cake cups. Decorate with sprinkles and cherries.

Ministrone Soup

1 lb shin beef – bone
3½ qts cold water
1 cup white or red kidney beans
1 tbsp olive oil
2 cloves garlic (chopped)
½ cup onion (chopped)
½ cup Parsley
Salt & pepper
1 cup string beans

¾ cup celery (chopped)
⅔ cup peas
2 cups shredded cabbage
1 cup carrots (diced)
1 cup tomatoes (diced)
½ cup macaroni
Grating cheese
2 beef or chicken bullions

Brown onion, garlic and parsley. Add remaining ingredients and macaroni last.
Simmer 4 ½ hours.

Anne's Pound Cake

½ cup butter at room temp
2 eggs
1 tsp vanilla
1 heaping tsp baking powder

1 cup sugar
½ cup milk
1¾ cup flour

Cream butter and sugar together, and then add eggs, milk and vanilla. Beat lightly and gradually add flour and baking powder. Pour into a greased 9" loaf pan. Bake 350° for 45-50 min. Cool before serving.

Zucchini Pie

3 cups thinly sliced unpared zucchini (about 4 small)
½ cup finely chopped onion
½ cup grated parmesan or swiss cheese
2 tbsp snipped parsley
½ tsp salt
½ tsp oregano
1 clove garlic chopped fine
½ cup vegetable oil
4 eggs slightly beaten
1 cup Bisquick® mix.

Mix together grease pan and bake about 25 min.

Good Morning Mom,

Today is May 13th, 2006, Mother's Day and I woke up excited because Joseph is taking me to Great Adventure! I'm excited, but something is missing. I miss being woken up to the smell of Sunday, the smell of garlic, browning meat for the gravy and bacon. "Mom, Happy Mother's Day in Heaven." This one is for you. Sundays were always special. Not only because we all went to church as a family, but because each Sunday started off with bacon, scrambled eggs and warm biscuits.

I didn't know it then, I miss it terribly now, but Sundays were Heaven on Earth because of you Mom, pure love.

Hi Mom,

It's been tough getting my heart down on paper to express how much I love and miss both you and Daddy. Boulders were thrown in my path every time I thought that I was finished. All pictures were rescanned at a higher resolution several times and Joseph, God Bless him, lovingly retook the more recent pictures. I believe the tennis match between me and the publisher have come to an end with the score LOVE – LOVE. I promised myself that I would not go to sleep tonight unless I finished the last request from the publisher. Today is May 8, 2011 Mother's Day. Happy Mother's Day Mom! ...with Love from #2.

End

I am the luckiest person alive. I won the parent lottery. Neither of my parents went to college, neither even graduated from high school, yet I believe firmly in my heart that they were the wisest, kindest, most loving people you will ever find. They were pure love. Each had their own unique way to demonstrate unconditional love and not ask for any thanks or money in return other than love and respect from their family.

Some of the most invaluable life lessons I learned from them have far surpassed any advice that I got from books or the far too many and far too expensive latest life guru's seminars that I attended.

Love life; live life; love everyone, and it's ok to tell them that you do the first time you meet them; love daily; respect your elders, and you must kiss them even if they have a cold sore which you will have for the rest of your life because of them; forgive, because we are not the one to judge; God made the person that way, they can't help it; we are not in charge, God is, so trust in him and his destiny for you.

Destino (Destiny in Italian) was a word they often used. So I guess on these days of destiny for my parents – Mom: July 14, 1921 to December 18, 1998 and Dad: May 19, 1918 to July 1, 2003 it was theirs.

Even the mention of their names or the thoughts of all the good each did brings instant tears to my eyes and opens the tear in my heart. I can't believe it. It's been over 10 years for Mom and 5 for Dad. In my heart I talk to them daily and in my soul I hold them forever, my mentors – my best friends – my parents.

50th Wedding Anniversary